A Chicken Named Ruth

-- a collection of true, amusing tales

*To Brenda —
What a gift.
Colorado Springs
turned
out to
be!
you are
a
joy.*

Linda

Linda Bryant Pulliam

A professional speaker, Linda Pulliam has spoken to thousands and thousands of people in hundreds and hundreds of places and had lots and lots of fun doing it!

A Chicken Named Ruth

-- *a collection of true, amusing tales*

Linda Bryant Pulliam

AHH CAPPELLA PRESS
Chapel Hill, North Carolina

To Charles

A Chicken Named Ruth -- a collection of true, amusing tales

Copyright © 1995 by Linda B. Pulliam

Portions of this book are heard during Linda's professional speaking engagements

Cover art wonderfully done by Kathleen Jardine © 1995

First Edition 1995

Library of Congress Catalog Card Number: 95-94087

ISBN No. 1-886951-05-5

Printed in the United States of America
95 96 97 98 / 6 5 4 3 2

Acknowledgments

Because of many people this book has at last come to be. There is no way to adequately thank everyone involved -- some are mentioned between these covers and many others not. A small handful does, however, deserve explicit acknowledgment:

Jeanne Robertson cautiously and gently and persistently badgered me to "put the stories on paper." Maybe this will get her off my back. Olivia Miller was ever ready with just the right suggestions. Hope, Louise, Martha, Sam, and Sue braved the first draft.

My parents have provided unconditional love and confidence in me from before my days in the Chinaberry tree to the present.

Kim and Charles, just by being themselves, are simply the best people anyone could have as family. They are also terrific material.

Contents

Preface

The characters in this book are real. And characters they are! Some more skeptical souls (no doubt fearing disgrace and humiliation) have been grudgingly granted an alias. The way I look at it, facts are facts and all the other parties contained herein will have to face public scrutiny for their assorted deeds. In most cases, I have supporting documents to substantiate my stories.

Telling stories is one of my favorite things to do. I've loved to tell stories for as long as I can remember. By itself, that's not a big deal but the fact is ... I'm also shy. It's true. Now you ask, why would a shy person intentionally choose to tell stories to a group of total strangers, none of whom are relatives and therefore beholden to her? It's beyond me. Still and all, it's what I do for a living. Since pretty many incredibly amazing things happen on a regular basis without solicitation, it's not necessary for me to make up stories. The events surrounding these stories are true.

I have transferred some stories that audiences enjoy directly from my head onto paper. My goal is to give you reason to grin or laugh and maybe bring back a good memory or two. In this humble literary effort you will find no life altering plan or get-rich-quick scheme -- just 100 chuckle-worthy tales.

Should you enjoy this fruit of my labor, then the countless hours of typing zillions of words, the

screaming and ranting, and near boxing matches with my beloved Charles will have all been worth while.
    Almost.

Cast of Characters

CHARLES (aka Chas or Chucko) - friend, husband, lover, confidant, and co-conspirator for many decades

KIM - #1 and only child

PAUL - #1 and only son-in-law

MOTHER - female parent who never gave up on me

DAD - male parent who never gave up on me

CAPITO - mostly Siamese cat*

DAISY - 100% beagle dog*

An assortment of wonderful friends who know my foibles and still manage to like me (a blessing for which I am eternally grateful)

* (both pets now liven up that great kennel in the sky)

Getting Started

Linda Bryant Pulliam

My First Audience

Past the corn crib, before you got to the pig pen, still well within view of the back porch, grew a splendid Chinaberry tree. It was right on the edge of my grandmother's back yard. One step past the drip line of the tree branches and you were in the field. Chances are, if you didn't grow up in the South, you've never heard of a Chinaberry tree. One variety of the tree, called an umbrella Chinaberry, is a small tree, barely more than an energetic bush. Even though the berries, when strung together, make smashing play-necklaces, industry has no use for the species. Chinaberry trees are good mostly for chickens to roost in at night and for little girls to climb for retreat from the summer heat and into their imagination.

Escape from the visiting female cousin was a widely practice sport among pre-adolescent males in the South during the 50's. I saw it played to an art form in my youth. The only girl among my cousins, I found great consolation in my Grandmother's Chinaberry tree.

On the fringe of a large yard, it was just far enough from adults to be an adventurous get-away. I now know, perched on a sturdy low bough of the tree, in a safe solitude I launched my speaking career. For hours I would amuse myself singing, mimicking adults, and telling stories to make-believe friends. And from that elevated vantage point my voice regularly attracted one red Rhode Island hen from the flock near the house. I would imagine that scratching fowl to be an adoring public gathered to hang on my every word. Her scratching for worms was applause to my ears.

I suppose she was my first audience.

Her name was Ruth.

Forestry or Oratory?

I'm often asked just how I happened to decide to become a professional speaker. The truth is *I* never decided. My aptitude tests in high school all indicated life as a forest ranger was my calling. Alas, khaki is not my color.

A lot of people are more than mildly intrigued by other fully grown people who are willing to make varying degrees of fools of themselves for a paltry round of applause and a dinner cooked by somebody else. The speaking seed may have been planted in the Chinaberry tree with Ruth, but it was watered during graduate school. Professional speaking was unknown to me at the time. I had never even *heard* of a professional speaker. For sure, if my parents had known one they would not have introduced me.

Required for a graduate course was a project working with different groups of institutionalized adults. I was to develop classes for the prison system, state psychiatric hospitals, and numerous extended care facilities. Well, what happened that semester was to affect my life for the next ten years. This project was great fun and immensely rewarding. My efforts ultimately evolved into a full-time job.

For several years I was a roving instructor, hauling flip chart, projector and assorted props to locations way off the beaten path. Then one day out of the blue, our big television station called and said they wanted to do a live "piece" on me and my innovative programs. HOT DOG! *THIS* is it. Barbara Walter's days were limited!

The TV producer told me to choose one of my *prize students* at the psychiatric hospital. We would be interviewed together.

On television.

Live.

Understandably, this decision required cautious thought. My television debut. Certainly the turning point in my career. Hello name in lights - good-bye flipchart.

It actually was an easy choice. His name was Vernon and he was my main fan. Vernon was the first thing I saw as I drove up to the hospital each morning. Waiting for me with his brown leather aviator hat, earmuffs sticking straight out, summerfallwinterspring. No doubt, Vernon would make me look great.

The TV crew arrived ... mobile unit parked out front of the main building ... electric cables snaked across the floor ... bright lights shone on people talking into high tech walkie talkies hooked to their heads. The patients lined up early for medications that day.

The producer put the interviewer, Vernon and me out in the day room on the genuine vinyl sofa. We were in full view of the camera's unblinking red eye. The interviewer asked "Vernon, what do you think of the programs Ms. Pulliam has been bringing out to the hospital for the past year?"

Then.

If I live to be 100 I will *NEVER* forget, Vernon turned, looked at me, looked straight at the camera and said

"I've never seen that woman before in my life."

You Do What?

Few have any idea what professional speakers REALLY do. Sometimes even I wonder. At a family gathering of a newly discovered batch of cousins, many of whom were many times more than once removed, I was introduced to the crowd.

"This is Linda, watch it. She actually wants you to *pay* her to talk."

No matter what you do, and no matter how long you do it, there are always relatives who mumble when relaying your chosen life's work. And eventually one of them will ask "Just how'd you get into that speaking thing."

Here's how.

Miller Harrison, a friend and colleague in need came to me with an urgent plea. Seems he had been assigned the responsibility of putting on a seminar.

"I can't do this alone" he said, "you have GOT to help me."

I reminded him that I had spoken to a group outside the psychiatric hospital and prison system only ONCE. We've all heard of those who can not lead three in silent prayer.

Begging and pleading, which rapidly progressed to threatening and menacing, he carried on. Then I started thinking, you know surely the *sum total* of my life's experiences are BOUND to be worth *something* to *somebody*. I owe it to society. I'll do it.

After practicing night and day, I could have done my part of the seminar in my sleep. (Charles claims I did on more than one occasion.) It was obvious soon into the seminar, I would not be heralded as an overnight sensation.

Is public speaking a recessive gene? It must be.

At the first break it struck me that I hadn't remembered Miller being such a distinct shade of gray when we arrived. He'd loosened his tie, unbuttoned his collar and generally relocated every hair on his head. He seemed quite concerned about something.

Have you ever spoken before a group and been so scared that you didn't know *what* you were saying? You were pretty sure that it was you that was saying it though, because you could look out across the room and nobody else's lips were moving. To compound matters, your subconscious chooses this precise moment to have a debate with your conscious with zingers like:

*"what in the WORLD have
you gotten us into?"*

> **"I DIDN'T KNOW IT WOULD
> BE THIS BAD!"**

*"How much longer is
this going to take"?*

> **"I'M TALKING AS FAST
> AS IS HUMANLY POSSIBLE!"**

Much to everyone's relief it finally ended. I found Miller, ran up to him and said "Well, tell me the truth. How'd I do?"

He said "Kid, if you would have had anything to say, you would have been dynamite!" Years later he told me my performance had made him physically ill.

Hard to put a value on friends like that. Years and hundreds of speeches later, Miller heard me give the keynote speech at a national convention. All he could do was shake his head and mumble "...the odds of this ever happening..."

Long Ago and Far Away

Linda Bryant Pulliam

Home Sweet Home

I grew up on the Gulf coast of Texas in a middle-class uniquely-Texas type of neighborhood. There were four house styles to choose from. The builder would move the windows around and use different colored roof shingles to try and trick the architecturally unsavvy.

Nobody was fooled.

We had one tree in the front yard. It never got bigger than the stake that held it up. If we'd had any compassion at all, we would have removed the stake and let the tree mercifully blow to the ground and call it a vine.

The house was so small, those inevitable, silence-filled, private, marathon telephone conversations of my youth necessitated retiring to my father's closet and sitting *on* his shoes. Dad never complained.

Instead of stemware, we had those aluminum glasses that start sweating as soon as you head towards the tea bags. Everybody knows iced Texas tea requires two inches of sugar in the bottom of the glass (non-optional). We also had the big heavy, multi-colored, currently trendy dinnerware that's required for California residency. Every night of my entire youth they were laboriously washed by yours truly. Totaling all the hours, I must have spent the better part of a year of my life at the sink with those plates. No time off for good behavior.

Growing up I can remember always having vegetation with some decorative mission on our dining room table. In a vase. No dirt. It wasn't *exactly* what you'd call a flower "arrangement." But it was real. Do you know how hard it is to *find* fresh flowers in the East Texas summer heat?

I drove past that house last year. There was a little girl in the front yard. Chances are, she has her own portable phone, a dishwasher and silk flowers on the dining room table. I'm glad I didn't.

Averill Elementary

I have an aversion to numbers and I don't need analysis to know why.

Back at Averill Elementary School I was the very last person in my 4th grade class to learn the multiplication tables. None too soon either. In fact, it was so late in the year I'm sure if you'd check my records there would be some footnote about it. (The records are under my maiden name.)

Do you have *any* idea of the lasting effect of being last at anything in the 4th grade! To this day, small "x's" even randomly sprinkled in and amongst numbers cause heart palpitations.

Before the tips were worn down on our new crayons, a proclamation went across the land...

*"You WILL learn these 'times tables' if it's the **last** thing **I** ever do."*

Learning the multiplication tables was a prerequisite for promotion to the 5th grade. Miss Hill's methods rivaled the rack. Few teachers are in my memory bank. Miss Hill takes up far more space than any one person is normally allotted.

Year 'round her black dress was anchored by a cameo pin under her chin and on her flip side, an ever-present knot of hair at the nape of her neck. Convenient for distinguishing whether she was coming or going.

Even 8x9 was required! <u>Perfect</u> recitation or NO promotion to the 5th grade.

"...eight times nine...give me a minute...eight times nine...it's seventy-two! or is it seventy-three? ...seventy one?" Oh well.

If for whatever reason, I am ever in a movie and cast as someone in sheer and uncontrollable terror, I'll conjure up this image in take one.

Fourth grade. Miss Hill, surrounded by brittle and yellowing times-table flash cards leering from atop the black board.

Cold sweat.

Heart rate accelerates.

Brain function slows down.

When time to come back to reality, I'd simply be prompted with those heart stopping words -
"SEVENTY-TWO"

Voila, an Academy Award performance.

Funeral Home Fans

Today's families are more inclined to move away from the home place than when I was young. Back then the families that "left" were thought of as either peculiar or adventurous. At any rate, "visiting the relatives" became a chance to check out other limbs on the family tree.

Every summer from day one until I left home, our nuevo-Texan family "visited the relatives" in Mississippi.

Those summer visits come to mind like a photo album rather than a home movie. Most of our "visits" were spent with my mother's family. They lived and still live way out in the middle of nowhere. Greyhound and Trailways do not even come to a *neighboring* community.

My maternal grandfather was taller than everybody. I didn't appreciate genetics but I did find myself feeling better about my height when we visited him. The man favored a balanced appetite for reading: half the time it was dime detective paperbacks and half the time his Bible. His fondness for reading was almost as great as his fondness for chewing tobacco. In fact, many of the relatives partook. Along with cousins, grandparents, aunts and uncles, Prince Albert was a familiar face during summers. It would take more than summer vacations for the Prince to grow on me.

My Grandmother looked exactly like Granny on the *"Beverly Hillbillies."* She was less than five feet tall, wore her hair in a country woman's bun and I believe she slept in an apron.

Pea shelling was a primary summertime activity in the piney woods of Mississippi. Women and children were the main enlistees. "Visiting" relatives were not spared. I have no earthly idea what the men did. Shelling peas was clearly never on their TO DO list. Their routine had something to do with getting in and out of trucks, sitting on the porch and calling dogs with great urgency.

Anyway, all pea shelling inductees were issued a bucket, wash pan or other large container. We were carefully instructed to "start shelling them peas!" There were no lessons and few rules regarding shelling and snapping. It was made clear quickly, however, that tearing the hulls open with your teeth was not acceptable.

There was never a shortage of dogs. One uncle had 18 hound dogs. All with names. Some with formal names, some with catchy names, some with custom-made names, and even some with dog names. Blue, Flop Ear, Judge, Queenie, and Bones come to mind.

Maybe I remember dogs so vividly because they were always in the middle of things -- AND my aunts would cook for them! Before dogs got picky and insisted on crunchy snacks packaged in store-bought bags with a canine celebrity on the front, they ate cornbread. Actually they called it "dog bread." Kitchen scraps and corn meal were baked in large flat, cast iron cake pans. The pooches were darn glad to get it too. Can you imagine serving "Winston the Jack Russell Terrier" a slice of day old cornbread. HA!

So much is forever in my memory bank from those summer trips . . . digging for potatoes with a spoon, cow bells breaking nocturnal silence, the rooster issuing an all points alert, a community water dipper, chickens that look you right in the eye, Jesus on funeral home fans, stand up dinners on the church grounds, year-round feather mattresses, sugar and butter biscuits, flour sack sun bonnets, and animals that earned their keep.

Sunday Dinners

Back before fat grams were discovered, people used to eat until they were "plumb wore out." Sunday dinner with *relatives* was an exhausting endeavor.

Red and white checked plastic tablecloths were adorned with massive blue-rimmed earthenware bowls and porcelain-covered speckled tinware overflowing with fried chicken, homemade bread-and-butter pickles, pound cake, cornbread, and Lima beans. Oh yes, the chocolate pie. Chocolate pie (Not mousse. Of course, not mousse.) with three and one half inches of meringue. It's a near extinct delicacy today. The health food nuts have all but driven it from the face of the earth. Thank goodness the pie still has a stronghold in some remote pockets of the Mississippi woods.

To let our pie settle, after dinner everybody whether they were deaf or not, would go sit on the front porch. We sat in chairs my Granddaddy made. The backs and legs were made out of small tree trunks. The chair seats once held a cow together. Don't think for a minute that Ralph Lauren invented those cowhide chair seats.

I can't remember anything we talked about. But it must have been OK with everyone because they've kept on doing it. The ones who are still alive do it to this day. I actually do too when I "visit the relatives."

Pre-convenience Store

My Aunt Reuta Lee lives in a very small, neatly dressed white country house at the end of a red dirt road. She grows spectacular red and yellow canna lilies in her painted white tractor tire. Red dirt must be good for cannas . . . that old white tire can't be good for anything.

Her pump-house appears held together by an ancient rose which has flourished for generations. It's huge. And when it's in full bloom you'd swear the rose was there long before the pump-house.

Aunt Reuta Lee had an entrepreneurial spirit. She was chief proprietor of a pre-convenience store. Her inventory consisted of your basic food groups -- white loaf-bread, Little Debbie snack cakes and Nehi, with snuff and chewin' tobacco found in the gourmet section. The store had a brick front, the kind of brick that comes on a roll of tar paper. The RC Cola thermometer that hangs in my kitchen today, hung *forever* by the front door of Reuta Lee's store. Over the years countless people started AND ended their day by that thermometer discussing the weather -- kind'a like the Weather Channel with a touch of good natured debate. I've often thought the Weather Channel would benefit from having two forecasters in dispute. Sometimes the weather just needs to be *talked* about.

Pickled Pears

A colorful floral curtain covers one complete wall of Aunt Reuta Lee's dining room. The house is not large, so right away you know "this wall can't have a window;" there's a window on two other walls in the room. Floor to ceiling behind this curtain are plank shelves filled with jars of beans, corn, peas, tomatoes and anything else that can be canned. My favorite jars hold pickled pears. There is nothing quite so delicious as a big, hot biscuit with *real* butter, topped with slices of pickled pears. Heavenly.

Sunlight deteriorates canned goods. That's the reason for the curtain. It's always pulled open for company and you can understand why. Green beans standing smartly at attention, bright red tomatoes looking like Christmas ornaments, and jars of tinted surreal green bread-and-butter pickles make one beautiful sight. Empty shelves are indeed a country woman's blank canvas.

A gardener par-excellence, Aunt Reuta Lee grew most of her vegetables. In gardening it never dawned on her to spray, dust or otherwise *scientifically* tend to her vegetable charges. One year there was a bad infestation of big black grasshoppers. Some people swear by them for fishing bait. Some people just swear at them.

She got "fed up w'em" and just went out to the garden one morning "and headed 'em off." Whooping and hollering at the unsuspecting grasshoppers, waving her apron over her head, apparently did the trick -- at least she still brags about the triumph. Ortho is no doubt glad that technique hasn't caught on.

Aunt Reuta Lee has always enjoyed eating as much as she does cooking. She's equally skilled at both. Once upon a time, she was quite thin. (For some mysterious reason, chocolate pie doesn't settle in the arms and legs.) Aunt Reuta Lee still has thin *arms* and *legs* as do all of the women on my mother's side of the family. A genetic reality of which I've made mental note.

Pie appears to have a distinct affinity for settling in the waist area. Aunt Reuta Lee declared the problem was with her belts. *They* just kept slipping up. Many summers of chocolate pie with 3 1/2 inches of meringue and my belt would have gotten confused too.

A Little Drum Roll

In Junior High School, I wanted more than anything to be a majorette. In order to try out for this very responsible position, you had to be in the band. To be in the band, you had to play an instrument. I didn't play one. Auditions were in September, it was May. I had the summer to become a musician. Plenty of time.

The triangle appealed to me. My father took me to pick up my instrument and sign the rental contract. Looking back, it was quite big of him not to say anything about my instrument of choice. Since his offspring would be the first musician in recorded family history, it's easy to see how he would have hoped for something more, like maybe a clarinet or a flute.

I practiced marching up and down the street, around the house, down the driveway and back.

Left, left, left, right, left.

So far so good.

Marching *and* hitting the triangle required more concentration. At the end of three months, I could read music, hit the triangle and march at the same time.

With this new talent, I auditioned for the band. The hours of dedicated practice paid off. I got in the band!

And most importantly, was selected for the majorette "team."

That first half-time performance, while I was marching across the freshly mowed football field, my father was in the stands repeating under his breath: "left, left, left, right, left ..."

P.S. I'll be in big trouble if I don't mention the majorette costumes. What our merry little troupe lacked in talent, we more than made up for with our eye-catching outfits. During my career in the world of batons, white boots and marching bands, my long-suffering mother sewed three quarters of a million sequins, seven miles of fake ostrich feathers and gathered enough ruffles to circle the globe. Twice.

Really Learning to Read

Up to my last year in junior high school I'd managed to dodge reading novels and almost every other reading assignment. At least cover to cover. After thumbing through the chapter titles, glancing at a paragraph or two, and then talking with friends in the hall before class, I had survived. Now, the end of another year was in sight and I was on a roll.

Luck ran out the day after returning from Christmas break. My English teacher! This bibliophile of the highest order was bound and determined to make us learn SOMETHING. (You know, they've **still** got 'em like that.) Her last assignment of the year required a book report. It wasn't even for extra credit. It must have been legal for teachers to give that kind of assignment back then, because she was sure doing it right out in public.

We had to *bring* the book to her and *tell* her *why* we had chosen that particular book over others. THEN *bring* the book in when we were half-way through and *give* our evaluation of the writer's style ... AND how we thought the major characters would develop.

Yipes! Crib notes weren't going to get me through this one. She had thought of all the angles. Recycled reports were out. Great Scott. I just might have to *read* a book!

Up to this point, the school library had basically been a good place to hang out in hot weather. It had big fans. After one summer in Texas, you know where the big fans are.

With the predictably of youth, I procrastinated until weeks before school was out. One afternoon, post-final-bell and pre-bus-boarding-time, I skidded sideways into the library.

Our school librarian was all alone amongst the stacks. Couldn't believe she stayed late on Fridays. My memory of her is of an extremely elderly woman *[probably late forties.]* She wore shoes with library-issue silencers in the heels. Instead of smiling, she had a hair-trigger SHHHHH. And I don't believe she sweated.

"Where are the small, thin books? I *have* to read one" I blurted. With sloth-like precision, she rose and motioned for me to follow. That's when it hit me ...

"I AM ACTUALLY GOING TO HAVE TO READ A BOOK."

She took me to a section and whispered, "This is all fiction and appropriate for teenage girls." After a quick scan of the shelves I announced that none appealed to me. She nodded. Fortunately, for me, she did have one *special* book that just might be what I was looking for. Once again, she motioned for me to follow. Back at her desk, she opened the middle drawer and pulled out a worn, burnt orange book.

The title was "Steamboat Gothic." With solemnity usually reserved for undercover agents passing secret information, she handed the book to me.

That night, after dinner, dishes, shower and the ritual hour with Uncle Miltie and the Texaco boys, I retired to my room. Waiting on my bed along with other school paraphernalia was THE book.

Page one.

The book told of a *beautiful young girl just about my age in the 1800's who didn't mind in the least wearing layers of substantial whalebone reinforced undergarments in Louisiana's 100 degree heat whiling away her days in the shade of live oaks dripping with Spanish moss surrounding the big white house majestically positioned on a rise overlooking the banks of the sleepy Mississippi uncontrollably falling in love with a talldarkmysteriousbroodingstranger who rode into the scene* fortunately in the first 3 pages....

I was snared. Before summer break, I'd escaped into most of the library's fiction *certifiably appropriate for teenage girls*. Of course this left little time for other activities like mathematics, civics and Texas history.

She was quite possibly the most significant person in my formal educational experience and I can't remember the librarian's name. Never even thanked her. Do you think she was satisfied with the "thank you" that came with every new book checked out on my library card?

So do I.

Starched and Ironed

Back before children ran the school system, *everyone* wore regulation gym uniforms. White, starched AND ironed. No designer label. Sizes ranged from XXXLarge to Mammoth. My legs appeared suspended from the elastic waistband.

Non-negotiable rule #2 was that *all* PE students were required to run the length of the gym while Miss Brown timed us. Bad yes, but (get this!) if the time wasn't "good enough" you'd have to do it AGAIN. If a blundering, knock-kneed kid couldn't run adequately the first time WHERE on earth would the energy and mental wherewithal come from for an improved performance!!!!!

The boys from the previous class used to sit in the bleachers and watch us. In this era, the authorities kept the boys and girls separated except for band and chorus. Hardly a wise policy to encourage relating with ease with the other half of the species. Imagine, running and dragging adolescence behind you the length of a gym, in front of a gaggle of snickering flattops. Darn near impossible to remember exactly HOW to run.

My "time" was never quite right by Miss Brown's standards. She would confide to me (while facing the boys in the bleachers) that I was the most uncoordinated girl she had ever seen. She even took the time to record her professional assessment on my report card. In ink. I still have it.

Professional assessments can stick with people for a long time -- making impressions that last well beyond the moment or the day. We must keep that in mind when we give one.

I can still remember occasions as a girl when I would attempt some minor physical feat. A well intentioned soul would say "Hey, you can't do that, you're too uncoordinated."

"Oh... Yeah... I almost forgot. Thanks for reminding me."

Later, as a young mother trying to finish college one course at a time, I needed a mandatory P.E. credit. Only a dance class was available

FLASHBACK!

Miss Brown and the gym.

On the first day of class the dance instructor came in to the studio, walked passed me and casually commented, "What wonderful feet you have. Your pointe must be spectacular."

Well. I became a dancer that day. I defeated the odds of a young adult entering the world of the ballet barre. Years of untold joy and a soaring sense of accomplishment were the result. One can only wonder what else might have been in the wings for me earlier had Miss Brown noticed my pointe...

Chunk

I was not in my element in high school. My style just wasn't "in." None of the primary youthful categories fit. Not "jock," not "artist in brooding," not "square," and certainly not "chunk." (For those under 45, refer to a high school yearbook between 1955 and 1960. Turn to the football season and find Homecoming. Homecoming queens are "chunks.")

In my mind, skinny was my main problem. Rubber bands held up my bobby socks. I've actually spent a good bit of my life trying to defy gravity and prevent articles of clothing from respecting gravity more than my various body parts.

While my legs were birdlike, my feet gave the basketball coach visions of how it would be in two years. (She hadn't heard from Miss Brown.) Ever the optimist, my youthful logic told me I could fool people into thinking I had more "petite" feet if my shoes were wider and shorter. We won't discuss IQ at this time.

Throughout high school, I proudly shared with an intimate circle of friends my shoe size - 7 1/2 B. What a difference several decades make; today my shoe size is 9 1/2 AAA. Remember, no discussion of my IQ at this time.

There are many disadvantages to being thin. I could never lay on my stomach while sunbathing in public or dance too close for fear of having my reinforced bosom indented. It was rumored that girls actually arranged for school transfers just because of one poorly timed indentation. It was just about my #1 fear from age 13 to 35. Of course transferring was never an issue for "chunks."

Wonder what they worried about?

28 AAA

Children are like dogs. It's a good thing kids are so darn cute when they're little because they can get to be so much trouble. By the time they become adolescents (*children* that is), they've been around so long, parents really don't see them as they are. We remember them as cute puppies. Well, you know what I mean.

As a kid (puppy stage) my cotton top was perpetually frizzed thanks to that amazing new beauty product - the HOME PERMANENT. Invariably my dress hem was out, sash flapping in the breeze, Fudgesicle tracks smeared across my chest, socks going down for the last time into my shoes. An all round charmer.

To the point, I was an unattractive child. Now, nobody actually came right out and *told* me this, but school pictures don't lie. The photographer would ask me to give him a big smile. Eagerly, I'd comply. He would then say "uh, maybe you could just close your lips *ever* so slightly..."

Clinically I had what is referred to as Dracula teeth. This is actually a rather common tooth malady. Dracula teeth are those funny little teeth located on either side of your bugs bunny teeth. Little pointy teeth. Mine were *veeerry* pointy -- stuck straight out as though trying to leave while the others had decided to stay. In fact, my upper lip rested on them. Cher had a very mild case of these teeth. Unfortunately, that's where our similarity stops. If Cher and I could stand side by side, both of us wearing very slinky outfits, your eye would first notice *my* teeth.

That was just the mouth.

The body, too, is worth mentioning. I come from a long line of people who eat with abandon and stay pathetically skinny until one day, fifty years of calories erupt at the waistline.

I was SO thin even people who were condemned to constant diets felt sorry for me. I've heard every "Skinny Minnie" joke in the book. Don't tell me another one.

Clothes on me gave the term *"socks on a rooster"* new meaning. Before pantyhose was invented, there were garters. Can anyone forget? I would knot my garters so tight, circulation to my lower extremities was temporarily altered. This self torture was futile for after two steps my stockings began their slow descent. I was totally devoid of surplus body mass.

People who grow up on the gulf coast of Texas spend a lot of time at the beach. I remember walking down to the shore, lying on my stomach on the soft warm sand, to watch the waves. I've always done that so well. And after a while, I'd get up, look down at two small depressions ... left by my knees. Then with an air of positive expectancy, I'd turn around and put my head where my feet *had* been. Talk about optimism! I've been hanging on to that optimistic expectation for about 35 years now.

When Kim was about 11 she wanted a bra. I told her *no way!* As was her custom, she went to her father. She asked Charles, "Dad, when did mom first need a bra?"

Without looking up from his paper, Charles responded, "Does your mother need a bra?"

Smoochin' at McDonalds

My first love was a handsome lad stretching to an imposing 5'2" with the aid of cowboy boots. I was a lithesome 5'9" on a flat surface.

This occasionally created a logistical problem. Indeed it was quite an accomplishment to cruise the local drive-in sitting very close AND low enough to allow him to put his arm around me (this was long before seat belts were a gleam in an engineer's eye.) Houdini would have marveled at my flexibility. I learned to both sit and stand in accordion fashion. To this day I can't reconstruct just how this was possible.

Everybody knows that love does conquer a multitude of obstacles. We would cruise for hours on end, around and around the local drive-in. No goal or mission other than to see and be seen.

Sort'a puts hanging out at the mall and smooching at McDonalds in proper perspective.

When "Hair" Was More Than a Sixties Rock Opera

The hairstyles of today's youth are really quite mild compared to those of other eras. Yours truly spent the better part of her youth immobilizing a Beehive by spraying it to chickenwire consistency while inhaling no small amount of the stabilizing mist. The shampoo-and-go-out-with-a-dripping-head style had not yet been introduced.

Maintenance for the beehive required rolling your entire head with toilet tissue and sleeping on your face. Small price to pay for beauty.

The male-equivalent hair expression of the times was the flat top. (I didn't run with the duck-tail crowd.) In lieu of spray, the fellows hiked up their hair with wax (as in wax-candles). Strategic hairs were held aloft by a not-so-thin layer of pink hair goo. I've forgotten the name of this essential grooming agent.

I vividly remember the sock hops on hot, humid Texas summer nights in the gym. At roughly a half foot taller than "my man" slow dancing meant his hair in my mouth or his mouth on the shoulder of my sweater. Oh the decisions. Laminated via hair spray to my heart throb for the Johnny Mathis selections, we'd sweat the night away. Those days, it really meant something to be "stuck on somebody."

Hair took a lot of energy back then. We all copied our styles from the movie stars. Marilyn Monroe was *it* in the 60's and consequently so was bleached hair. I reasoned, with the same color hair as Marilyn, *probably* I could trick people into thinking we had other similarities.

The first time I bleached my hair it broke off at my scalp. Oh yes, and it was green. A head scarf was standard attire for two months. Only a minor glitch in the never ending quest for beauty.

Can't say I ever recall being mistaken for Marilyn. Must have been because her tint wasn't *Frivolous Fawn...*

Tell Me Again

Whenever my mood monitor registers blah, yuck or generally morose, it always lifts my spirits to have Charles tell me the story about the first time he saw me. (Feel free to use this story if you think it will make you feel better some day. Use your own names.)

When it came time to choose a college, my family was faced with some real dilemmas. Basically it came down to who would enroll me for the money we could afford and house me where my parents felt I'd be safe at night.

#1 There was little evidence at the time that I would turn into the sterling individual I have become. Which is to say, no schools were actively recruiting me. (My brother was accepted at Harvard, MIT, Stanford and

Columbia. Full scholarships to all. WHEN HE WAS FIFTEEN.)

#2 We couldn't afford most of the schools that actively recruited those students who were not being actively recruited by anyone else.

In the end it came down to the University of Texas and Louisiana State University. It was important to my parents that I reside in a bona fide dormitory residential setting. Those were the days when self respecting parents felt it crucial that their daughter be locked up at night by a dorm mother who slept with the keys around her waist.

LSU had women's housing available.

Texas didn't.

I went to LSU.

I was the very first person to move into the Nora Neil Power Dormitory on the LSU campus. Today it's no longer a maximum security unit. GUYS even live there these days. In those days all the skinny pines surrounding the dorm didn't reach the second floor windows; today they have been replaced with great tall trees. Amazing how they did that.

Registration before the days of computers was very low-tech as you might well imagine. It was the first challenge of college and took place in a large, open field house. Folding tables were scattered around the gym with signs hanging from the rafters - ENGLISH 101, MATH 220, SPANISH 1 ... Glassy-eyed faculty sat with boxes of punch cards, each one representing a seat in the class. Cards gone; seats filled; class closed. That's that.

According to Charles (and it *is* his story) he had been watching me across the gym and following me through the maze of tables for more than an hour. At last, standing in the same line, he was preparing to make his move. Never mind that it was WOMEN'S TENNIS 101.

The card box emptied and the line scattered. Charles was devastated.

The story gets downright cosmic at this point.

Billy (who was Charles' roommate) and Karen (a new buddy of mine) were best friends. Destiny. The two of them had already decided to get us together. Billy cornered Charles on the way back to the dorm and asked him if he wanted to have a blind date with a *really swell chick.* Charles already had a date. Billy said "Too bad, cause there she is standing over there."

Here is where I make Charles go real slow.

Charles looked across the gym, saw that it was the girl of his dreams (and Women's Tennis 101). He told Billy, "I'll break my date."

Our date has lasted thirty years so far. And when the year rolls over to 50, I'll still be asking Charles to tell me the story about the first time he saw me.

Repossess the Baby!?

When it was MY turn to be the mom we were in luck. I had given it some serious thought and had the routine figured out. I was prepared to sail through the process. No sweat.

Right.

Actually, I was still operating under this delusion for the first several days after Kim was born. At that time you were expected to stay in the hospital for four or five days after delivery. When the baby needed to eat, someone would bring her to me. When I needed to sleep, someone would get her and take her back to the nursery. Like I said, no sweat.

My first inkling there might be more to motherhood occurred the day we brought Kim home from the hospital. It was then that I realized I did have just a few questions...

Like:

Is this normal poop?
Did she get enough to eat?
Will I die if I never sleep again?

There truly is a guardian angel for new mothers who don't know which end is up. She basically lets you know early on that one end of the baby gets the food and the other end gets rid of it. You wing the rest.

Kim weighed 5 pounds when we left the hospital. This was back when that was a tiny baby. Because we didn't have insurance and we were a pretty all-round pitiful student/parent combo, they let us take Kim home early with one stipulation. Before release from the hospital, she HAD to drink 3 ounces of formula at a feeding.

New babies drive a hard bargain. She had no way of knowing that she was being paid for in installments. Repossession had a perilous ring to it. We had to get her home.

Meal time meant milk in her nose, both ears, coating her cheeks and throat area. Babies *just might* absorb nutrients through their skin. I was covering all the bases. It worked and we all went home.

After a month, our Doctor insisted she take 5 baby spoonfuls of rice cereal twice a day. It's harder to absorb cereal through the skin and even harder to convince a new baby of the value of trying to do so. She hated cereal. I thought she would become Barbie sized if she didn't eat ALL FIVE bites.

Meal time was traumatic. There was wailing at both ends of the spoon. I'd slide in a morsel or two during a big mouthed gasp for air. Gurgling and choking, out it would come. I'd cry some more. So would she. After mealtime, we both had to take a bath to rid our exteriors of rice cereal AND to calm our interiors.

Sure wish I'd known then that she would someday grow up to be on a perpetual diet and live for days on rice cakes! It would have saved us both a lot of tears.

First Pet

Nina, a yellow Labrador Retriever, was Kim's first pet. Even when it's tough making ends meet to feed three mouths, a pet can bring pleasure worth far more than the cost of rations. Labs take a ton of rations, but Nina gave every bit back in family entertainment. (Pets were a lot cheaper before they routinely started expecting to be fitted with dentures, hearing aids and pacemakers.)

As is predictable with the breed, Nina was a chewer. She would chew furniture legs or garden tools. It didn't seem to matter much to her. For a long while Nina's chewing on things didn't bother Kim very much. In fact we were aware of how *our* rage with the dog seemed to even tickle Kim. Maybe it was the only evidence Kim had that she wasn't at the end of the family pecking order. Finding humor in the dog's bad habit ended abruptly for Kim the day she discovered Nina snacking on the feet, hands, and bosom of her prized Barbie doll. Kim was inconsolable.

I don't know how much you know about Barbie dolls, but when they get nibbled on their permanently arched feet, red fingernails, and cleavage they depreciate considerably for the 6 year old market.

This nibbling habit, as it turned out, put only a temporary strain on the relationship between the child and the dog. Kim soon discovered that Charles' dirty athletic socks were more tempting to Nina than

Barbie's precious parts. All she had to do to divert Nina's attention from her play things was to offer Nina one of her Dad's gym socks. Try to get the sock back and a rough housing tug-of-war ensued every time.

And like Barbie, gym socks too depreciate in the jaws of a labrador retriever. Multiple holes in Charles' socks guaranteed him to act the age of his own child.

Fleas on The Tooth Fairy?

Kim's first loose tooth experience is now in the family archives. We've got it on home movies.

She was proud of this most visible sign of maturity. Of course, a "big girl now" accolade is something you cling to dearly in those early years. She would not let us pull the tooth. Even as it hung by a thread of skin, flapping with each word she uttered, she wouldn't let us touch the tooth. After a while, we became worried that it would fall out and she would choke on it. (One of those fears handed down from generation to generation. Recorded history would show such an accident's chance of happening is somewhat on equivalent to a meteorite falling on your bed.)

The truth is, the dangling tooth was gross and we had to do something. The home movie camera had become a fascinating family toy, no doubt contributing to our daughter's still evident theatrical streak. Horsing around just for the camera, being silly with Dad behind the lens, was big sport. We were always thinking up silly schemes to film so the "trap" was easily set once the camera came out of the bag.

I suggested to Kim that we tie a string around the loose tooth and hang something from it ... oh, say, a NAPKIN RING. Hey, this was getting interesting. Kim was sliding into the mood at this point while Chas and I were straining to maintain our composure.

Since this was being filmed, there was a sense of high drama about it all. Kim has been a ham since she was about, oh I'd say, three years old. Anything was worth considering for a chance to get her mug in the center of the camera. We were all laughing uproariously at the sight of Kim with a napkin ring dangling from her tooth.

Don't get ahead of me.

As soon as Kim was thoroughly engrossed in her performance for the camera, I pulled one of Charles' gym socks through the napkin ring. With Kim dancing around the room, I let Nina into the room.

The camera rolled.

You guessed it.

Nina saw her sock, swinging enticingly from her best friend, heard our laughter, and her doggie brain reasoned "party time!" Nina came tearing over to Kim, grabbed the sock and ran across the room with the first extracted tooth as a bonus.

Kim told her friends at school that her dog pulled her tooth. Of course nobody believed her.

This is the part *nobody* will ever believe. Nina pulled Kim's second tooth also. We have it on film. Watch for us on the funniest home movie show on TV. I already know how I'm going to spend the money.

The Good Old Days ...

Remember when young people left home to venture into the big, wide world with a snack for the road, maybe a new pair of shoes, and some letters of reference. It was all they needed.

Leaving both of our parent's homes with next to nothing, Charles and I moved into a condemned garage apartment over a crumbling foundation on a busy thoroughfare close to the Louisiana State University campus.

It was not for rent when we spotted it, and for good reason. The construction was at best "temporary" twenty years earlier.

It just wasn't fit for dwelling. But the location was right, and we needed a place to stay. So in the typically tough negotiating style of college students, we made the owner an offer. If WE could resurrect the apartment to a standard the city would approve, he would let us take up residency for a mere $50/month!

The owner agreed, and we were thrilled. Now let's talk specifics.

There was a spider-web covered stove in the kitchen. The stove had one working eye. To use the oven, we had to prop the oven door closed with a broom that was wedged under our cinder block bookcase in the hall. We had to be SURE whatever we were cooking was done because once we kicked that broom away from the oven door, there was no replacing it. Broom handles get hot!

The bathroom window never fully closed at the top. The shower head was absolutely inflexible ... frozen in a spray path to suit a basketball player. When the water pressure was turned on too strong, more than a little sprayed over the shower curtain and right out the window. In order to keep most of the water in the tub the pressure had to be so low it would take fifteen minutes to rinse off the soap. In November, fifteen minutes with the window open, even in Louisiana, is a looooong time to rinse.

One week after Kim moved into her first apartment, we were informed that she simply could not get by another week without a microwave.

That First Real Home

Somehow, living above a garage didn't instill that sense of home for us. It wasn't until a year later when we moved to Monroe, in northern Louisiana, that we experienced the joy of our young family's first home.

Oh, the wonderful memories. This first home was actually a duplex that had been converted to a dwelling from a WWII aircraft shipping crate. Yes, you read that correctly. Our house had once transported partially assembled airplanes. We lived on one side and our landlady lived on the other. It was The RITZ compared to the decaying garage apartment.

With only twenty-four hours to find a place we moved boldly and quickly. The rental ad said:

"Duplex, no children, no pets, no students..."

Undeterred, we drove up to the listed address in our 55 Ford with a screaming two year old, yipping pooch and registration packet for classes starting the next week. I've often wondered what made that dear woman change her mind. Once when I asked her, she simply mumbled something about never having seen anything more pitiful.

Weather in northern Louisiana is usually quite mild. If converting shipping crates into apartments in 1943, I don't think I would have invested in insulation for them either. Exterior shingles to keep the rain out, and interior wall board to "hide the secret" probably made sense for a unit that wouldn't be needed beyond The War.

One day in the midst of a particularly energetic cleaning frenzy, I moved our bed several feet closer to the wall. The next morning when our alarm went off at 3 AM, Charles (newspapers to deliver) leapt from the bed feet first. This was a sure wake-up routine when that extra wink could be disastrous.

Both feet, flying from under the sheet, landed in the front yard. Yes, through the interior wall and the exterior siding. *Steppin' out* took on a whole new meaning that morning.

Summers *more* than make up for mild winters in Louisiana. In summer we relied on an attic fan to survive the heat. It was so loud that when it was "on," all conversation ceased. You couldn't have heard a plane land in the driveway. We communicated with hand gestures. This fan came in handy when Kim entered the tantrum era. I'd turn it "on" and she'd shut up. The kid wasn't stupid.

Need I mention we were on a limited decorating budget? Still, we wanted to brighten up the baby's room. Fifteen yards of unbleached muslin at ten cents a yard, a 15 cent box of crayons, and my creative genius was unleashed. I made simple cafe' curtains. Each window had a theme. On one section I drew an alphabet motif. On another, smiling-faced vegetables and fruits were dancing about. Kim would stand at the end of her crib, tiny little finger pointed at the curtains saying "appull, gwape, nano."

When we moved, all sophisticated and ready for bigger and better things, the curtains went to the thrift shop. I think I would even surprise myself at the check I'd write to get them back.

Off!

Some children are easily embarrassed when they don't already know how to ride a bike, jump rope, shoot baskets, etc. They want desperately to be able to do these things, but they don't want to learn in front of anyone.

Near our first home (the airplane crate) there was an old swing set with a swing-glider. I don't know the correct name, but two people ride facing each other and use their feet to "pump" to gain speed and altitude. The ride goes back and forth the same as a swing.

Kim was about four years old and had watched the older children through the fence for quite a while. One day, she sneaked from our yard, setting out to conquer the contraption.

Soon I realized she was missing. A frantic search lead us to the playground.

Functioning as both pilot and co-pilot, she had gotten airborne with no problem. After who knows how long of frantically pumping the mechanism, she'd had enough and didn't have a clue as to how to stop. Apparently she had been in a holding pattern for quite a while, for her little legs were so shaky when we finally rescued her, she couldn't stand.

Such is the way with many of life's lessons. We just have to get on and have faith we will figure out how to get off.

Oil

We bought our first car for $65 -- CASH.

The cash part was key as I recall. I also recall the seller as a rather nervous fella who kept looking over his shoulder throughout the transaction. Any person who has been around the block at least once, knows that a $65 car probably has a very interesting story behind it.

Standard operating procedures for this first major family purchase consisted of stocking 3 quarts of oil on the front seat, with a string-held can opener suspended from the gear shift. Charles could tell when it was time to add a quart by the color of the smoke in the rear view mirror which was, by the way, nailed (yes, nailed) to the car roof.

Parking on a slight downgrade made starting easier -- actually it made it possible. One year later, we sold the car for $25 scrap metal. And it only cost $10 for them to come pick it up.

Three weeks after the car was gone from our lives, we got a notice for an overdue payment. We had forgotten, we'd just bought new tires for the car and had eight more months to pay on them. Oh, life's lessons.

We have a spiffy car now. At least there is nothing nailed to the roof. I still don't know what all the bells and whistles do. The dashboard looks like the control panel of something nobody in our family has a license to operate.

For the longest time, I thought the battery check light on the panel was a skull and cross bones. The more I think about it, glasses might be a good idea on a more full time basis. Some pretty important things go on inside the car too.

When it was still new, the back window somehow got cracked open just a hair. The wind noise was driving me crazy. I tried every button on the panel except the skull and cross bones. Finally I stopped at a gas station and asked the attendant to see if HE could possibly figure out how to get the window up. He walked around, opened the back door and rolled up the window with the manual crank.

The car has heated seats. Imagine. This discovery was made one very warm day shortly after we had gotten the car. I was late for an important meeting. To set the stage, glasses aren't actually *required* for me to see other cars when I'm driving. Now when it's necessary to see what's going on *inside* the car, it's another story. I need them.

My glasses were resting on the counter at home. Somehow, I had unknowingly turned on the seat heater. It was impossible for me to see the panel controls enabling me to eliminate the slow roasting that was taking place on my dorsal surface. The only other option was to turn the air-conditioner to sub zero creating a comfort zone for at least half of me.

You know what the man at valet parking was thinking that hot July day when he parked the car, sitting on my heated seat with the air-condition blowing full blast.

Hormones...

42 Regular

Shortly after Charles and I married, we applied for a charge account at a major department store. Naturally, the application requested our sources of income. We listed birthday gifts, found money, and even selling blood. Unfortunately we no longer had an account with the tooth fairy.

So impressed was management with Charles' attitude, they offered him a job. He was assigned to men's clothing. Minor hitch. Store policy required *all* salesmen wear a suit. Second hitch. Charles didn't own one.

As fate would have it, there happened to be a blue suit that had been returned with a hole burned in one of the pants legs. The coat was a 44 short (Charles wears a 42 Regular) so the big-hearted department manager was willing to sell it to us at a greatly reduced price.

Hired!

Charles worked at the store for an entire year. Every day before work he would take a blue magic marker and color his leg under the hole. That still seems the best solution thirty years later. Fortunately, he never resolved the coat size discrepancy. I'm pleased to say he has kept his youthful figure and still wears a 42 regular.

The department store job was only part-time, so we needed another source of income. More good luck! The newspaper had an opening for not one but TWO delivery routes. Our financial picture was looking up by the minute.

Soon we held the distinguished title of "newspaper distributors" for a 1000 customer route. We were at the loading dock at 3:30 every morning.

> quart of oil - *check*
> can opener - *check*
> parked on incline - *check*
> baby on floorboard - *check*

Kim had to come with us. We adhered stringently to the child labor laws of the time. No work for the baby. She cooed and gurgled on the floor of the back seat watching me roll and snap rubber bands with the flair of a pro. Charles still laments the lost art of tossing a paper out a car window over the roof to hit the sweet spot at the foot of a front step. Although he no longer has a paper route, I'll bet he could still do it today. He's a college professor now; perhaps he could practice by throwing test papers back to his students.

We delivered to a lot of elderly people on one of our routes. One man (we never saw him) would leave a nickel in his mailbox ... IF he wanted a paper. If NOT:

no nickel. His mailbox was up 43 stairs. After one year of doing this daily, we received a 10 cent tip.

Another customer was a woman who was always up when we made our pre-dawn run. She and her nondescript mutt would be sitting on her porch waiting for us. The routine never wavered. She would come out to the car, check on Kim and produce a penny lollipop from her apron, have us pet her dog and then she would tell us what the weather report was for the day. After this ritual, we'd say we had to go. She would step up on the curb so we could turn our car around. As we pulled away, she would walk into the middle of the street and wave good-bye as if beloved relatives were leaving after a long visit.

Where Were YOU?

On the first day of school a faint YAAAAHOOOOO can be heard spreading from cities and hamlets across the land.

KIDS ARE GONE! TIME FOR ME!

Oh, what learning years. For both parent and child alike. Kim arrived in the 60's so naturally she had a part-time hippie mom. Hippie only in appearance, mind you. I've always been somewhat conservative and in my twenties I didn't know enough about the world to have a real opinion on politics or the economy.

Like so many others of my generation, it was imperative to "find myself." I searched in pottery and modern dance classes, graduate school, discussion groups, community consciousness-raising enclaves, and in our organic garden.

A little of me was in all those places. Charles fortunately had never been lost so he just patiently waited until I was fairly certain that the me he'd known all along was the real me, or at least the me we were settling down with.

It's unfortunate that mothers today must (or feel compelled to) go right back to work after baby arrives. There are so few times post-childhood when women can explore, examine and expand personal horizons quite like the years when they're the home based anchor for the family. It's true that by business community standards, home management counts for zip. However, the books I read, the classes I took and the people I met during those years have made me a far more interesting and marketable person today. Rather than my brain turning to mush during this era, I discovered I'd been thinking and doing what everyone in corporate America was dreaming about.

Certified Parents

Having grown up in the "straighten up and fly right/don't look at me in that tone of voice/snatch you bald headed..." period of developmental child psychology, I decided to perform MY parenting routine from a thoroughly *sound* scientific position.

This revelation came to me about the time Kim started school. Classes abounded for those who wanted to be on the cutting edge with their parenting responsibilities. Perhaps you too are a graduate of one of those parental training programs.

Of utmost importance was the child's psyche. The child's psyche was fragile and not to be tinkered with. Everything must be explained to the child in *great* and tireless detail. Choices were given in all areas. Even for punishments. Kim was allowed a hearing if she felt the sentence too harsh. Negotiations were encouraged for age-old family rules. This worked *really* well for ... a *really* short time.

One particularly exasperating day Kim had been certifiably obnoxious and in response to one of her 20 or so whining harangues, I told her:

"ZIP IT UP AND DO WHAT I SAY BECAUSE *I* SAY SO, THAT'S WHY KIDDO!!!"

It slipped out, just like that.

Oh no.

Injured psyche.

Permanent damage.

Ohdearohdearohdearohdear.

Shortly, she seemed fine. Could it be that all this time she'd been wanting me to draw a line in the sand so she could go on to other things?

Sometimes things don't need an explanation. Sometimes if you are the little one, you've just gotta do what the big one in charge says.

After love and devotion have been well established, discipline need not be such a big problem.

Don't YOU look at me with that tone of voice!

What's Changed?
Motherhood or the Germs

We have a young friend with four kids. They are all under seven years of age. This cheery clan maneuvers around town in a station wagon with the rear bumper affixed to the main frame with a twisted coat hanger. Mushrooms grow on the floorboard of the back seat.

Even without advanced training in animal psychology, you recognize immediately that their basset hound does not come from a long line of dogs named "Sir" somebody or other. This sterling specimen of the canine community is named Einstein. Einstein has one friend. It's a parrot named Placido. Placido "summers" in a huge cage in his fenced yard which is adjacent to Einstein's fenced yard. Placido squawks and Einstein howls harmoniously for impromptu performances throughout the day. To the best of my knowledge they've never actually played together, but they are clearly colleagues of sort.

The baby seems none the worse for eating Einstein's snacks. After being partially gummed then carried around in a clenched fist, they do at least *look* a little like teething crackers.

The older children are quite adept at hiding cookies under sofa cushions for future retrieval. This I have heard is quite the norm in multi-children families. I wouldn't know.

Like young mothers everywhere, our young friend gets a bit frazzled from time to time. Late one afternoon I dropped by unannounced and was greeted in the driveway by Tina Turner blasting from the stereo. I got to the front door, looked in the window and saw our friend dancing and laughing wildly with two of her older children. Odd musical selection yet the children knew all the words.

The baby who was too young to dance was sitting on the sofa eating what looked like Einst. . .

Linda Bryant Pulliam

Long Ago ... But Not So Far Away

When We Get To Greensboro

Moving has GOT to be one of the most exasperating events in an average human lifetime. Just in general, we don't take kindly to having our nest upset. Nothing about the process is comforting. **Nothing.**

Have you ever moved on a cool, sunny day with ample time, the right size truck and plenty of friends to help? See what I mean?

When our young family finished school -- *the first time* -- we headed for Greensboro, North Carolina. With our meager belongings packed in an off-brand rental truck, we couldn't have felt more adventuresome had we set out on the open seas. This illusion was pretty well gone by mid-afternoon. No air-conditioning. No disposable diapers. No "leisure" money to make the trek from Louisiana to the outer reaches of the "South" a more pleasant experience.

We had enough money to stay on the road one night and keep the rented moving truck two days. This was before it was permissible to pull a car with the rented truck. Charles and Kim drove the truck and I followed three feet behind them in our aging Ford. Forever imprinted in my memory is our little caravan pulling over to the side of the road in Kannapolis, North Carolina for a brief moment of hysteria. That's where I unraveled. Kannapolis. Not bad, I waited all the way from Louisiana.

Of course this whole exercise was new to Kim, so she didn't know how to react ... until she saw Mom. Then she took her cue and Charles had to try and console both of his babies. Tears spent, he and Kim loaded themselves back into the truck and I crawled into our trusty Ford for the final leg of the trip.

Incidents that once seemed too big to handle in our youth are so inconsequential in the spread of life.

Our battle cry then was "when we get to Greensboro..." THEN and only then, *normal* life would truly begin. No more school, no more student housing, actually enough money to start paying back school loans.

Well, once we finally got to Greensboro, you know what happened. Our impoverished student woes were replaced with a whole new set of challenges.

Today when Charles and I are unduly postponing enjoyment until *everything is taken care of* one of us will say "when we get to Greensboro..."

The truth is, we humans never get where we're going. Projects are never tidied up to complete satisfaction. Precious time continues to speed by with no regard to our personal agenda. We all are waiting "until we get to Greensboro." Our destinations are all moving targets.

We must ENJOY THE JOURNEY! ... even the stops in Kannapolis.

Fruit Cake

Granny never actually *asked* if we liked fruitcake. They just kept coming. Every Christmas. Year after year Granny would give us a really *big* fruitcake. Somewhere, someone is bound to like fruitcake.

One year during our starving student days this annual "treat" arrived at a particularly lean financial period. Dinner time rolled around and there was nothing in the pantry except a few potatoes, some tea and ... well, a very large fruitcake. I served a slice that night as the main course for dinner. Next day - no financial improvement on the horizon. You guessed it. Fruitcake for breakfast, lunch AND dinner.

To make a very long story short, for *four* days we ate fruitcake -- candied pineapples, cherries, dates and all. It seemed to never end. On that fourth day it still looked big ...that's how really big it was, or how tired of it we had grown.

Fortunately we weren't called upon to make any binding decisions with legal ramifications, for I'm sure we were somewhat wired after ingesting all those altered fruits. To this day when offered fruitcake during the holidays, Charles and I share this *sweet* memory.

The first Christmas after Granny died, a fruitcake arrived. She placed her order a year in advance to make *sure* we got our prize.

Christmas has many modern-day symbols across the land (e.g., wreaths, decorated trees, eggnog, wrapped gifts). We enjoy them all, but the one that is most special at our house is ... yep! FRUITCAKE.

Justice!

Remember when a youngster would act up in church? NO debate. Mom would take the errant child by the arm and make a hasty retreat. Invariably this meant crossing in front of the entire congregation. This was done with nary a hint of remorse on the mom's part. Nobody blinked an eye. Justice was being served.

This will date you. Remember the cry-rooms at the movies? Society used to incarcerate youthful offenders in public places for MINOR infringements such as whimpering during a strategic moment in the movie. It was grounds for instant banishment. Reprieves were unheard of.

Somehow there has been a shift of power. On the cereal aisle in every grocery store in America you can hear -

"Mom, can we buy this cereal, huh Mom, can we? Hey, there's even a free, get it Mom a **free** whistle right here in the box. THIS cereal is actually saving you money. And after all it's good for bones, you do care about my bones don't you mom? Calcium right here in this box. All this for under three bucks. Let's hear a big yeeeeees from the old Mom . . . Mom, I won't be quiet until we get this cereal!"

Do you think there could be a market for cry rooms for parents?

Caged Capons

Until I was a full grown adult I thought going to the State Fair was one's patriotic duty. To the best of my knowledge, *I* went to the State Fair every year of my life from birth until I was 20 years old. From our vantage point in the little one horse town where I grew up, the fair was the only taste of the world afar. Anyway, we always went.

After Charles and I had been married a couple of years, I was stunned to realize that he did not share my enthusiasm for this annual event. In fact, he assumed he had seen his last Fair. I couldn't believe it. The man had a serious flaw in his patriotism and *he hid it so well*. He soon reformed and family trips to Raleigh for the North Carolina State Fair became an annual event.

Caged capons were always a big draw but the major reason I'd go to the fair was to endure those stomach churning, head reeling, no-brainer rides ... and get thoroughly nauseated all for the price of a ticket.

Everybody has a favorite ride. Mine always was and still is the **ROUNDUP**. Centrifugal force for heart stopping fun. One of the major BCC rides. (BEFORE Cotton Candy)

The **ROUNDUP** is a show and tell lesson in physics. First of all, you ride strapped in, *standing up*. Imagine a Ferris Wheel pushed over onto its side. Slowly it starts going around and around. Then it starts picking up speed and tilting. Eventually it gets to an upright Ferris wheel position. By this time more than a few ticket holders are screaming and reconsidering the wisdom of this choice.

People wait in line and pay good money to get to do this.

Charles wanted no part of rides once Kim outgrew the merry-go-round. Kim and I promised no more rides -- after this one. He reluctantly agreed.

Kim was apprehensive, but what child can refuse a ride your mother wants to go on. The ride was almost full when we got on; we couldn't find three places together so I stood across the ring from them. The motor started. *S-l-o-o-o-w-l-y* we began whirling around. I could tell Kim was not elated and was seconds before crying. I raised my hand to give a comforting wave when centrifugal force kicked in. Instantly my hand was pulled down - SPLAT - onto the thigh of the man next to me.

I could NOT move my hand. By this time nobody could move a muscle. We were all stuck in whatever position we were in.

The stranger cut his eyes downward toward my hand in horror ... and struggling to reach for my hand to move it, he realized why I hadn't.

A quick glance across the ride at Charles and Kim showed expressions frozen in disbelief. Kim mouthed the familiar adolescent cry --

"*MMMMMOTHER!*"

Charles just kept darting his eyes from the man's face to my hand.

The centrifugal force continued to grow. I could barely speak out of the side of my mouth, but I did manage to apologize to the man for the duration of the ride.

State Fair

Charles had to acquire a taste for the State Fair ... but he did. Mostly, it was cotton candy and the agricultural exhibits that finally won him over. They give away a lot of interesting things in those agriculture exhibits. Once he came home with an entire booklet that showed in full color photographs, how to raise emus for fun and profit. It's still filed in his bookshelf downstairs under investment potential. In case you don't go to fairs, emus are tall birds that look a lot like Big Bird. They don't talk or have agents though.

Fully half his time at the State Fair is spent signing up for those drawings that promise valuable prizes. He secretly thinks he's going to win a working farm one of these days. I don't have the heart to openly question this expectation.

Chewing on a tasty piece of straw, with his boot hiked up on a bale of hay discussing select farm issues, *carefully chosen so that his greenhorn status will remain a secret,* he invariably has an all round grand time. You see, Charles doesn't have many opportunities to talk about soybeans at the University of North Carolina Pharmacy School where he teaches.

Each year he also scours the midway looking for those booths that **GUESS YOUR AGE**. Thanks to the fact that he looks like a nominally aging paperboy, we are the proud owners of some perfectly delightful collectibles such as fuzzy dice that fit any size rear view mirror, a shocking pink stuffed rabbit and matching custom embroidered felt hats with "Stud-Chuck" and "Linda Babe" across the brow.

Charles hyper-ventilates in the presence of these traveling age-guessing professionals. He always wins. It must be similar to the "high" gamblers get when they know they have a winning hand. The *professional guessers* are always off by at least eight years.

These days, selecting his prize has become the challenge. We have run out of tacky friends to give these one of a kind prizes to. You know what my main fear is? An Elvis wall hanging. We don't have one. We don't have a tiger on black velvet either. These two items would complete Charles' State Fair collection.

Once, while ambling towards a guess-your-age booth on the midway, he turned to me, looked up at my gray hair, and not wanting *me* to *give him away...* he whispered, "Blend in with the crowd."

Zoie

Zoie has been a good friend for over 25 years. Our lives brought us both to Chapel Hill, North Carolina on the same July day.

She and her husband, a psychiatrist, have 6 children. I have never known of a time when there wasn't a broken bone, stitches going in or coming out, or one of their borderline-civilized four legged beasts in trouble with the local authorities. In fact, they once had this dog named Quasimoto. He would get nabbed about every other week. Quasimoto was used to the routine. Whenever he'd see the dogcatcher's truck, he'd jump right into the cab and drive around with him all day, then wait at the canine lock-up until someone would post bail.

Once Zoie's husband was walking home from work. Neighbors were standing in the yard watching the fire truck that was parked curb side. Without even breaking his stride, he asked "What did Zoie do?" She had set the kitchen on fire while frying chicken.

One day Zoie and I were having the equivalent of a quiet lunch, with dogs barking, doors slamming, cars squealing in and out of the driveway, and the dishwasher clanking for a little background music. All of a sudden, for some reason there was relative calm. Then Zoie and I heard the most mournful, eerie, inhuman cry imaginable. Both of us ran to the door thinking, oh my goodness ... who this time?

It wasn't coming from outside.

We followed our ears to the kitchen. Our eyes landed on the dishwasher at the same time. Zoie flung open the door and out stepped the most miserable looking, drenched to the bone, disoriented cat you've ever seen. All his hair was going in the same direction. HE'D GONE THROUGH THE PRE-WASH CYCLE!

Zoie turned to me and screamed, "What are we going to do?"

I said, "Don't ask me, we don't keep cats in the dishwasher!"

She decided a call to *"the expert"* (her psychiatrist husband) was indicated.

The receptionist said he was in a meeting and couldn't be disturbed. Zoie said *this* was an emergency. Knowing the family's track record, the receptionist wisely put her through.

Zoie frantically explained the situation.

Are you ready for this? The man is paid BIG bucks for his opinion. People drive from far and wide to find out what he "thinks." He said, "Dry the cat off, Zoie."

"Dry the cat off! Oh yeah, yeah, that's it, sure, thank you. That's what I'll do, dry the cat off." Zoie hung up and then turned to me and asked, "Do you think I should run the dishes through rinse again?"

How Much Will "Free" Cost?

Chances are your children or grandchildren are currently taking lessons of some kind. Talent or no talent, it's the American way.

You give your children lessons whether they have *any* talent or not. Our daughter can play one $1,440 tune on the piano. That doesn't count gas money or the value of my time waiting. Four years of driving year-round through rain, sleet and 110 degree temperature and waiting in the car under those same conditions for the duration of the lesson. One song! One! It's not even a particularly good song.

We do however believe in the American way. Over the years she went on to take:

1. voice
2. guitar
3. magic
4. violin
5. horse back riding
6. gymnastics

(While previewing a rough draft of this book, Kim added ballet, jazz and flute to the list.)

Thanks to these experiences, today she can jump over a fence with a horse IF the horse is so inclined, execute a nominally amusing card trick and almost do the splits. These skills rarely impress during employment interviews.

We were not totally witless during this pre-prodigy era. Never once did we consider installment payments enabling us to place a Steinway baby grand in the middle of the living room. "Until we were sure what to buy" we propped an old upright piano against the basement wall.

The ad in the paper that caught our eye said

"FREE - delivery included
Upright Baby Blue Piano
No guarantees No return

It had been hastily painted *Carolina Tar Heels* blue by an enthusiastic, musically inclined fan. It had all the earmarks of a previous fraternity house life.

Although we had moved up in our lives, we had literally moved down. Our first shot at home ownership was on a lot that descended on a 25 degree slope away from the street. Of course, this made delivering this "free" piano a breeze.

For quite a while this collector's piece was a real conversation starter. It certainly was "one of a kind." Several months into this episode, we remained oblivious to what would unfold.

Soon it became apparent that we were not producing a Van Cliburn challenger. The piano had to go. And then the real irony struck: "No guarantees No return." The FREE delivery was *down* hill; the pick up would be in the other direction. Giving the piano to the next hopeful parent with a "FREE -- delivery included" was going to cost us a bundle.

To shorten the agony of this story, suffice to say there simply are no readily available disposal methods for a musical baby blue elephant. We cut the piano up with a chain saw. The legs and wood sections were buried behind our compost heap. We paid two young weight lifters to carry the heavy metal innards up to the street.

Imagine the faces of the trash pick up crew. What did they think? Bad lesson? Long suffering neighbor heard the scales once too often?

We learned our lesson well. As parents we're off the hook. Charles and I can NEVER be held accountable for the premature termination of any of Kim's creative and artistic endeavors. NO guilt can be tossed our way when she sighs and wistfully regrets not being a musician, dancer, or world class horsewoman. *We have written releases.* In the attic is an entire notebook filled with documents signed by Kim AND witnessed. These documents clear us. SHE wanted to quit. WE agreed to pay for lessons as long as SHE would practice. SHE could quit at any time. When SHE wanted to quit, WE got a termination release. It's all right up there in the attic.

Just as legal as legal can be.

For Animal Lovers Only

If you are not an animal person, skip right over this story.

Before having pets of our own I never understood what people meant by "we aren't cat people..." or "we're not into dogs..." I really didn't get it. Now, having intentionally shared my house with furry things at my feet, I get it. You are either willing to spend a sizable chunk of your kiddo's inheritance on nutritious crunchies in 50 pound bags, squeaking mice, vet bills that would go a long way towards a face lift ... or you would never in your wildest dreams consider it.

I love animals. Something is missing without little beasts underfoot to chatter with when no one else will listen. (Maybe it goes back to Ruth.) I like cats *and* dogs. Actually, I don't *really* dislike gerbils and white mice...

Forget what I said about the rodents.

We've all heard that the only real difference between cats and dogs is the method they use to raze your house. It's either chewing or scratching. One method just takes a little longer than the other.

Charles grew up with a big German Shepherd. He never had a cat and didn't want one. He was more than slightly uninterested when I brought home a ball of kitty fluff.

One of Kim's classmates had just returned from a year split between Germany and Italy. We were all impressed to hear this nine year old, tossing out phrases in TWO different languages. She informed us that the German word for *curious* is Capito and since our new kitten operated in a nonstop discovery mode. It was a perfect name, Capito.

As a bratwurst devotee, I should have questioned the lack of a Germanic ring to Capito. Oh well, we liked the idea. Months later our young friend admitted she had made a slight mistake. Rather than meaning curious in German, it seems Capito is actually slang for something like *"all right already, I get it..."* in Italian. Too late, Capito had already established a credit history with his name.

Capito was a Siamese cat except for his tail and one leg. As he got older it became apparent that he was linked genetically to at least one striped ancestor.

Charles said it was all right to have a cat, he just didn't want anyone in the neighborhood to know that it was *ours*. He announced, "Nothing personal, but I simply don't want to be around the cat." Somehow, Capito got wind of this. So, for weeks he would sit with cat diligence outside Charles' office. One day he ventured a tiny cat step into the room, with ready access to the established escape route. Then, day by day, we noticed that he was moving closer and closer to the easy chair in which Charles perched most evenings. This planned attack amused us greatly. One day Capito, in slow motion, inched to within striking distance of Charles. Even cats know timing is everything.

The next evening Kim and I peeked in and saw Capito sitting in Charles' lap. I don't know which was the more enjoyable to witness, Charles holding his paperwork aloft to accommodate his new associate or the unmistakable expression of feline triumph.

Who says cats don't smile.

A Life Saver

After we'd had Capito for about a year, one evening we went to bed without cleaning up after a dinner party. One of the votive candles on the table was accidentally left burning.

In the middle of the night I was awakened from dangerously deep slumber by Kim's cries. Capito was sitting on her chest pushing his feet into her face.

Our dining room table was on fire. Flames were leaping towards the ceiling and there was a great deal of smoke. We were all slipping into unconsciousness. Only Kim' cries roused me. And that was with great difficulty.

The fireman said we were minutes from having the floor on which we were sleeping engulfed in flames. Standing in our front yard, watching the firemen spray water into our house, one of them remarked that we were very lucky.

Charles said "*Our* cat saved our lives."

For the next fourteen years, Capito was a bonafide member of our family.

Where's The Cat?

Once, while taking Capito to the vet for his annual checkup, I made one quick stop along the way. Arriving at the vet, I realized much to my horror, Capito had bailed out at my earlier stop! The car door had been open for only a second, but just long enough for him to escape.

Running into the vets' office I cried, "I've got an appointment, but my cat's not here!"

Being unnecessarily cute under the circumstances, the vet said, "Perhaps you should come back sometime when the cat can make it."

I panicked. Went back to the neighborhood where I had stopped earlier and knocked on every door. No sign of a cat stranger. Distraught, I called Charles and told him Capito had vanished into thin air.

It's a good time to tell you about Daisy. She was our innocent looking beagle. We got her the same month we got Capito. [CALL ME BEFORE SERIOUSLY CONSIDERING a BEAGLE FOR A BONEFIDE PET.]

For their entire lives Daisy and Capito had a love-hate relationship. The love component was a bit hard to detect sometimes.

Charles is the logical thinker in our family. (You can at least act like that's news to you.) He suggested that since Daisy was a hunter, just maybe she could track down Capito. It was worth a try.

We went home, got Daisy and took her to the unfamiliar neighborhood. We piled out of the car and gave Daisy the old "Where's Capito? Go on Daisy, get the cat ... get Capito ... sic him Daisy ... good dog ..."

Soon Daisy *seemed* to act like she knew what was happening. She *seemed* to know it was showdown time. Being encouraged to track down that spineless cat, surely she wondered: "Could it get any better?" As the reality of the moment crystallized, in beagle-like fashion she put her nose to the ground. She soon stopped right over the sewer lid in the middle of the street.

Capito was in the sewer! I yelled "Charles, get in the sewer." You must remember, this is the same man who once wanted a public disclaimer regarding cat ownership. Reluctantly, Charles removed the sewer lid and lowered himself into the subterranean unknown.

The story ended happily.

Capito lived to see his hair turn gray. Everyone was happy except Daisy. She spent the remainder of her life waiting for another sanctioned time to tear Capito apart and see what made him meow.

Heavy Metal

Adolescence. Remember three earrings in one ear? How about black fingernail polish and Heavy Metal music? Baggy shorts with boxer underwear hanging out the leg holes. Delightful stage.

Routinely the family witnesses hormones uncontrollably backing up and then surging forward. Lest this not be bad enough, he/she is sure the world is against him/her. Sound familiar?

1.   "Boys/Girls don't like me"

2.   "I'm ugly/fat/skinny/short/tall"

3.   "There's nothing to do..."

What would happen if we told the truth?

Response to statement #1

Very perceptive. It IS hard to like you right now but the family has great hope that you will soon outgrow this stage.

Response to statement #2

You would look a lot better wearing clothing more closely linked with those deemed by the bell curve as, normal.

Response to statement #3

Your agenda does seem somewhat barren. Perhaps you could spend just a little time learning potentially useful social skills like how to eat in public, utter a collection of words without ten of them being "like," and locomote without the aid of a life support system called Walkman.

And if none of this works try:

"Just go sit in a tree and talk to the chickens. It might do you some good."

"Homesick"

If you have a child or children over the age of 19, you know he/she/they think nothing of dialing home in the middle of the night to check in, ask for money, or cry on your shoulder.

As an exchange student in Europe, Kim regularly called at the cheapest time for *her* which was in the middle of the night for *us*. Predictably, this nocturnal scene went somewhat as follows:

Exceptionally loud phone ring at 2 AM. Over our now equally loud heartbeats, we heard a transatlantic cheery "Hi Mom 'n Dad. What cha' doin?"

Stateside, our response "Oh, nothing much. Dad and I are just hanging out in bed waiting for the wake-up alarm to go off."

Then (according to our rehearsed scheme) we'd immediately call her back to save *her* **our** money. Of course, we were creating a financial flow that would make sense only to parents of generation-X children or the Federal Government.

Routinely her call was to announce she was:

1. **A bit low on cash**. However, she's *pretty* sure she can wait a couple of weeks to get the prescription filled, *after* she gets paid. This would be the same child from whom we had received postcards from Paris, Berlin, Salzburg and Milan in the previous month. Actually, a choice between cough medicine and a croissant on the left bank is not a tough call. We'd make the same decision.

2. **Painfully homesick.** The pain can be lessened only by some of her grandmother's, family-secret oatmeal cookies. This bit of nostalgia converts to a request for a box of cookies at approximately $30.00 a dozen, not counting the labor.

3. **Overcome with gratitude for our wisdom.** Jolted from peaceful slumber to be told we are no longer out of touch with reality. What a miraculous transformation we made, even as we slept! (It also proves they have beer in Europe.) That's good for another $50.

What would you do? Natch. We're waiting in the parking lot when the bank opens the next morning. For starters, a twenty dollar check gets a couple of hundred dollars headed towards Europe. And upon receiving this "loan" Kim then pays who-knows-what to turn our money into the coin of the realm.

Having completed this financial interchange, while walking home she is overcome by a vendor's bouquet of tulips and the euphoria of youth. She plunks down a fistful of the newly acquired cash, and clutching her bargain she walks up the stairs to her apartment with pocket change. I'm not sure where the $25 phone bill fits into this international equation.

We think she learned this in college, but we're not sure whether it was in Economics or Marketing.

House Rules

During a recent Thanksgiving dinner at my parent's home, I asked my mother to pass some of her famous coconut pie. She told me to eat my carrots, *then* I could have dessert.

"Thanks," I responded, "but I am currently not interested in these carrots. What I need is some of that coconut pie. A big slice please."

With little eyes, mother said, "you are not setting a good example for your child."

"The *child* is almost 30 years old! *I* qualify as an antique at flea markets in 50 states! *I* believe *I* should know when it's time for carrots and when it's time for coconut pie, for crying out loud."

She stood firm.

Rather than cause a scene, I ate a few token carrots. "NOW may I have some pie?" Digging into my well-earned treat, I asked Kim if she wanted some pie also.

"Nope. Mema gave me a piece before dinner."

Imagine!

Have faith in the kids. All of them; even the weird looking ones.

When our daughter was 21 she didn't live at home anymore ... that is, unless she was sick or had no food. Today she's married with her own lovely home and a very successful career in Atlanta.

We still, although not often, miss those *crazy* post-childhood pre-adulthood years. Kim and her friends would descend upon us before going out on the town. We had usually been in bed about two hours.

I clearly recall one evening when a crew came over. They were dressed to party. This one kid had on a T-shirt with HUGE red lips on the front, Bermuda shorts with, yes, underwear hanging out from the hem, short Henna tinted hair standing straight out all over, high-top basketball shoes...and this was a girl.

Today the young woman is an attorney in our Nation's Capitol.

The Gate Agent

Deciding what you want to be when you grow up is never easy. At least, in earlier times, the options were fewer. The quandary was mercifully limited in scope. Just think of the list of potential professions that weren't even *invented* one measly generation ago.

Kim was interested in advertising from an early age, so we got into the habit of collecting interesting ads for motivational purposes. Once on a flight I saw an "eye-catching" ad in a magazine on the plane. You've probably seen it. It was for Perry Ellis men's underwear. An impossibly handsome lad with a perfect physique is casually sitting on the beach in his skivvies, creating no apparent stir. No stir on the beach, that is.

Without a moment's hesitation, I ripped the page out, folded it and put it in my airline ticket folder and promptly forgot about it.

On the next leg of my trip, I approached the gate agent and gave him my ticket folder to process my boarding pass. He pulled out the magazine ad and unfolded it while looking for my ticket. The smile filling the lower half of his face revealed his find. My immediate response was to start frantically explaining why I had torn it out of the magazine. Explaining that there was a legitimate reason for it being in my possession.

He continued to smile saying "Don't you worry one bit. I'll just put this right back here where you had it, nice and safe, and you can get to it real easily."

I bet the people waiting behind me wondered what could possibly be in the ticket folder of the woman in 3A to have caused her face to turn such a bright shade of red?

Hey, equal opportunity for "Dirty old ladies."

MIL

We always wanted a son. So when Kim and *perfect* Paul set the date, we were ecstatic. Our announcements read -

Linda Bryant and Charles Crenshaw Pulliam
announce
the arrival of a son
Michael Paul Schouest
August 19, 1989
This new addition weighs in at 185 lbs and stands 6'2"

For the time being, he calls me MIL. That's short for <u>M</u>other-<u>I</u>n-<u>L</u>aw. Isn't he clever?

Because of a special economic opportunity (one of them got a job) they had to move the wedding up 6 months. It sent us all into a tailspin. Every morning as soon as her feet hit the floor, Kim would be off on a quasi-frenzied tangent.

One day I said "Kim, you have got to get a grip. When we are planning such an emotionally charged event with friends, family, enemies coming from far and wide, you'll just have to own up to the fact that SOMETHING is going to go wrong. Admit it and be willing to laugh about it..."

Tears from her face hit my face.

"You are just *HOPING* something *HORRIBLE* will happen at MY wedding, so you can go all over the country telling your stupid little stories about it."
And I have! Read on.

Planning the Wedding - Family

We have a lot of friends, family and assorted people who have been part of our lives for a long, long time. Many of these dear folks wanted to be involved in Kim's wedding production. But there ARE only a finite number of roles no matter how creatively you stretch it. Even when you add understudies, there just *aren't* that many parts to play.

We were locked in for the bride and groom, immediate family and a North Carolina delicacy for the reception -- Bill's Bar-B-Que.

My suggestions for casting soon were being routinely ignored. I'm pretty sure Kim's attitude began shortly after I suggested Nikki the toy poodle-in-law (related to Paul paternally), wear satin saddlebags and carry the rings. What a memorable addition it would have been. People would have talked about it for years!

Kim said that's what she was afraid of.

Planning the Wedding - Rules

It took a while for Kim to realize the wedding would not be America's answer to one of the royal family's *events*. Unlike Queen Liz, I had an alternate/cheaper plan for almost everything.

Example: **Engraved** invitations. I tried to reason, "Kim, there are processes available today where *only another printer* would know whether they are engraved or not..."

Example: "Hey Mom, I've got a much better idea, one you'll *really* love. Why not go down to Quick Copy Center for the midnight special, run off a couple of hundred copies and stick 'em under the windshields!"

Clearly, the stress was getting to her.

Hmmmm. I wondered. Do all her friends ever park in the same general area...

Planning the Wedding - More Rules

Wedding protocol is tricky. The slightest oversight can create a ripple effect that will never merit forgiveness.

Every wedding planning book tells you *the bride's family is responsible for coordinating and color coding: clothing, food, parties, favors, church, clergy, flowers (in stands and on people), announcements, invitations and thank you's.* This of course is not to mention the weather, emotions, and second guessing everything in between.

Family and friends were coming from far and wide, including Europe, with many not having seen one another for years. Or ever. The occasion was going to celebrate a union and a reunion, so we settled on a monthly newsletter to keep everyone informed about the plans and planning going on in Chapel Hill. This way, even those who had never met anyone else in the wedding party, would know a bit about "who was who." It also served to lighten up a potentially hairy time.

In one letter was a cartoon of a young groom saying to his bride "And to thee I give my worldly possessions." In the congregation, the groom's dad leaned over to his wife and said "Well, there go the skis."

I howled when I saw it. Then suddenly it wasn't funny at all.

You Gotta Do What You Gotta Do

A few years back, Charles started making mumbling noises about building a house. I didn't pay much attention to him and before I could say "two-by-four number-two-grade pressure-treated southern-yellow-pine"* he had gotten all the permits and had broken ground. We were in the home construction business.

I asked him *"what on earth makes you, a college professor in <u>pharmacy,</u> think you can build a house!!"*

Indignantly he responded,

"Now just one minute. I got a book from the library."

At this quick response I couldn't help but wonder ... persistent optimism or academic naiveté'?

When I say *build a house,* I'm not talking about sitting in the comfort of an air-conditioned contractors office, looking at doorknobs and wallpaper books. I mean actually doing the plumbing, wiring, and insulation -- the whole bit. Once we were committed, we were committed.

Naturally, I wanted to do my fair share. Well, I didn't exactly *want* to, just decided it was "help out or go back home to my parents." It's hard to believe we put together a house. I don't even like puzzles.

Charles said, "Not many people do this...."

It soon became all too clear why.

We were definitely a team. Laurel and Hardy come to mind.

Being limited in skills but wanting to show my support immediately for this harebrained endeavor, my first inclination was to tidy up the work site. Charles' tools had never been properly organized. I was not a moment too soon in this project. Stretching to be logical, I figured it would be best to organized them according to purpose.

Turning tools: screwdrivers, wrenches in one bin.

Pinching tools: pliers, C-clamps, in another.

Cutting tools: saws, wood chisels in still another.

We now had a system in place that anyone could comprehend.

That initial input set us back a minimum of two weeks, IF you're to believe Charles.

* (2x4 #2 PT SYP) if you happen to be into framing

Gopher

Someone had to be the gopher. Charles owned all the ladders. The gopher had to be me. In my official capacity, I went to our local builder's supply store, contractor sales as my destination. In a booming voice, I informed the salesman "We're gonna need us a bundle of 2x4's."

The salesman asked "...how long do you want em?"

I said "Oh, no, you don't understand, we're going to have to *keep* them. We're building a house."

Downhill momentum picked up at this point. A legend in the making...

On another trip to the supply dealer, while waiting in line to be served, a very restrained although obviously "intense" voice on the other side of a wall petition said " *Look buddy, I've had that woman ever' day this week. I'm telling you, today she is YOURS!*"

My fate was sealed for all eternity when I asked for a carpenter's apron. Size 8.

This fellow finally did come around. He became my buddy. You'd think he would have felt some sense of accomplishment, seeing my progress during construction. One day I came to the store with a list of questions and supply needs and discovered he had suddenly resigned and was going to attempt to walk across some mountain range. Tibet I believe it was. Guess he felt he could do anything at that point.

Oh for the days our only power tool was an ice cream maker.

Cecille

If you've ever built a house, you know there are some things that you start out wanting ... but you don't get. And then, there are some things you get that you had not planned for. Nor would you *ever* have planned for them.

I didn't want a kitchen. A shelf with a string of outlets down one wall would have sufficed nicely. The resale potential alone should have made us jump on this idea. Charles was unwavering in his plan to have a kitchen. Scientists are so inflexible.

This was an educational project. Today, I know a lot about wiring. I really do. For your information, there are three ways to wire an outlet -- two will kill you.

I now know a whole lot of things like that. Wasted brain space.

Throughout it all, there was Cecille, a good friend and confidant. She flat out told me that she would NOT help me with any hammering and nailing. Wailing and pleading would be to no avail. She did however, give me permission to cry on her shoulder **once** a week. Best offer I'd gotten.

On one therapeutic visit I bawled "Cecille, oh Cecille. *This* may be it. *This* may be the very thing that pushes Charles over the brink. The man stayed up just about all night finishing the plumbing. And there is hot water in all the toilets."

She looked at me and said, "I see. Linda, just one question. What prompted you to check the temperature?"

Will It Match My Eyes?

Our do-it-yourself era was coupled with a back-to-nature phase. We have a farmette. Charles also fancies himself a gentleman farmer. In the midst of all this turmoil in my life, the first of my *significant* (emphasis is on the *significant*) birthdays rolled around. I had gotten down to my fighting weight for my mid-life crisis, for what might be that *last charge up the hill,* and I NEEDED a sports car. I didn't just want, didn't think it would be nice to have. I NEEDED a sports car - BAD!

Everyone knew. Hints were well timed and heavy duty.

The big day arrived and after a romantic candle lit dinner on our partially finished deck, Charles said "Honey, come on out to the shed. I've got a little surprise for you."

I could hardly contain myself. Why, I could just see me cruising around town. The only question was - would it match my eyes?

"Stand right there and don't peek." Charles instructed. I heard the shed door creak open and then, the most gosh-awful explosion. Bewildered, I looked up in time to see Charles drive out in a full-size farm tractor.

I burst out crying. Proudly he said, "I knew it, you *really* like it don't you!?"

Oh, the significant gifts that have been bestowed upon me. Would you believe I own a chainsaw with a custom carrying case. Yep. *And* a candy apple red roto-tiller with "LINDA" on the fender. The man is absolutely clueless.

After I had spoken at a large banquet, a woman levitated from her chair and frantically worked her way through the crowd. She came onto the stage, ran up to me and said,

"I believe we're married to the same man!"

8,745,932,551 Rocks

In assigning "jobs" while our house was being built, I somehow got the dubious honor of being in charge of our road or what city dwellers call *the drive*. People with a bit more poetry in their lives call it a lane.

Our road was originally underneath approximately 100 scrub pine trees, untold miles of honeysuckle vines, and an occasional stretch of rusting barbed wire wrapped around rotting fence posts. Charles said "Use your imagination!" What he really meant was use your new chain saw.

Clearing the land proved to be baby stuff compared to obtaining the gravel for the drive. Ever been to a gravel pit or a rock quarry? Why do I ask these questions, of course you haven't. Quarries are where the rocks for non-paved roads come from.

The memory of my first trip to the quarry is a keeper. I told "the man" we needed enough rocks to make a road. He didn't appear to be too interested in just what we wanted the rocks for. Mostly he wanted to know the amount. Determining if I have a pound or a pound and a half of bananas stymies me. My response was "Oh, how about 8,745,932,551 rocks..."

They sure hire some cranky people at rock quarries.

After the gravel for the drive was ordered (divine intervention was how we arrived at the amount), delivered and laid, we needed some pea gravel for the walk. You likely don't know what pea gravel is either. It's pea sized gravel. I didn't say you couldn't guess, just that you probably didn't know.

My order was too small a load for one of their big trucks to deliver so I had to go back out to the quarry and get it myself. I arrived at the gate, shovel and bucket in full view. Guess how often women arrive at a rock quarry with a shovel and bucket. Rock quarry by definition is a major hole in the earth with large trucks driving around *in* it. These trucks are getting loads of rocks for projects like regional water reservoirs, airport runways and foundations for skyscrapers. A woman and a bucket?

Check-out at a quarry means getting in line with trucks loaded with TONS of rock. Everyone gets weighed coming in and then leaving. My load was approximately 100 lbs. Please note here that I (*me alone, Linda, writer of this book*) loaded 100 pounds of rock from the earth into the bed of our truck. ME.

I asked the check out man if he would weigh my load with me in and then let me hop out of the truck so I could see what I weighed after all that exercise. There must be something about quarries that makes you real irritable after working in them for a while.

Not So Long Ago

Linda Bryant Pulliam

Significant Birthdays (aren't they all)

This past birthday was another significant one. I was counting on something universally considered appropriate for a significant birthday. Off on another delusionary tangent.

Waiting in the driveway when I returned from running errands on the afternoon of this celebrated event, was a large box. My immediate guess was that it harbored something useful.

Charles was beaming. I've come to recognize the smile that says, "I chose it myself."

I feared the worst.

All women know to be wary of gifts that can't fit into an evening bag.

I immediately ruled out diamond earrings. Perfume shouldn't require such reinforced packaging. I'd already gotten a garage opener.

With a well rehearsed act of anticipation - I tore into the box.

Would you believe it. Never would I have guessed in a million years. For this most-significant-to-date-birthday, Charles gave me a COMBINATION leaf mulcher and wood chipper. Top of the line. Hey, there's more! There was even an EXTRA bag to hold the results of chipping, shredding and pulverizing. The bag IS only guaranteed for ten years. Sure hate to be caught without a back up bag.

I was a bit surprised the chipper came without headlights. Should one get a hankering to do a little chipping, shredding or pulverizing in the middle of the night, what *would* you do without a full moon?

Leisure?

The people who know these sort of things say gardening is the undisputed #1 leisure activity in the USA.

That comes as no surprise to me. Anyone who has made an emergency zip to the feed and seed store on a sunny Saturday morning when the soil is just beginning to warm up also knows, gardening is NOT a pursuit for the faint of heart. Nor is it for sissies.

People can't load their cars fast enough with bags of sterilized$^{(?)}$ manure, good bugs to annihilate the bad bugs, and shiny shovels.

These folks are on a mission.

Growing up in Texas cattle country, it's still a mite hard to grasp *paying* good money for bagged manure. An enterprising entrepreneur in (where else) California advertised renting cows by the week. They were billed as "...environmentally safe grass cutters with fertilizing capability..." Winning combination.

We have always gardened. I'm pretty sure when Charles and I were gazing deep into each other's eyes during our romantic courtship, we never discussed shovels and fertilizers. Wonder how it ever came up in the first place? Hmmm.

Anyway, many seasons have passed since the early days of tomato plants in old laundry baskets strategically placed on our roof. The first year we moved to the country we planted 125 tomato plants and 50 hills of potatoes. For city slickers that doesn't mean much, but for anyone who has ever hoed a 50' row, your gasp of admiration is acknowledged. Need I tell you, we didn't know what we were getting ourselves into?

Our garden was, for years, the envy of our urban friends. We never had any luck with corn though. The raccoons watched us plant it the first year and word rapidly spread across the county.

Chapel Hill is a very environmentally conscious community. We'd probably be run out of town if we tried to buy an air rifle. Most likely deported if we seriously harassed a raccoon. I shudder to think what would happen if we *considered* doing one in. There was no limit to our creativity or expense in trying to keep them away. Scarecrows ... rubber snakes ... live-humans menacing and taunting. All to no avail. Raccoons are dedicated, unflappable scoundrels. They don't pick up on hints. We put a portable radio in a plastic bucket placed on its side, turned the radio up real loud and waited for the raccoon-repelling music to take effect. Amazing discovery. Raccoons *like* Country music. In more ways than one, we live on the edge of civilization.

During this most unsuccessful musical experiment, we had friends visiting from Germany. Sitting on the porch one evening I told Charles "You better go turn on the radio for the raccoons."

Our German friends didn't say anything. They just looked at each other with an expression that said, "Oh well, they *are* Americans...."

It doesn't take long to learn about certain crops. For example, I once heard a man say that you learn everything anybody ever wanted to know about squash the very first year you plant it. He was right. First of all, just like he said, it does taste amazingly like its name. (Trying to jazz it up with a handle like zucchini fools nobody.) And second, regardless of how many plants go in the ground, even the sorriest gardener ends up harvesting three times what friends, relatives AND an occasional stranger passing through (raccoons included) can possibly eat.

It would save a lot of time and travail if only there were regulations regarding squash. A solitary gardener with more than a six pack of squash, would trigger an alarm system.

The law of the hoe set is - if you grow it - *you've got to get shet* of it*. Lord knows you can't eat it all. You can fool people with zucchini bread only so long. And pickled squash. Come on. Oh, the pressure throughout the ages on farm wives.

Take heed you neophytes. Mid-summer, in any public area such as around flea markets, park benches, and church parking lots, you may happen upon a plain brown bag with the words FREE TAKE ME. You're looking at a bag of squash. (Zucchini, maybe. No matter. Remember squash is squash.)

* For urban dweller readers "shet" means get rid of.

Male Drivers

Historically, there have been far more gender jabs directed towards women drivers. Charles, along with the rest of the male subset of the species, has somehow reasoned that men are unquestionably the *expert* driver. Cosmicly deemed so, at that.

Interesting, for I (representing the other subset):
• have never gotten a ticket

• never had an accident

• RARELY have people with large veins
     in their necks speak to me from
     passing cars

Charles has had experience with all the above. With some regularity, I might add.

On long trips he drives; I navigate. However, he consults with me only when we are two car lengths from a sign that says *exit only* or *no turnaround for 30 miles*.

THEN he wants to know "Quick, which lane do I need to get in?!"

As you might imagine, on some occasions I don't respond in the nanosecond required and then we're doomed. Doomed and jinxed for the rest of our ingenuously planned trip. Ingenuously planned by you know who.

I've driven in 44 states. I've never been permanently lost. *My* ego allows me to ask directions.

It's been said the world is divided into two groups of people.

1. Those who ask directions, and
2. Those who drive around in a perpetually clueless state trusting loosely harnessed hormones rather than someone who has lived in the area for 27 years.

Passing the same street corner for the seventh time it seems so logical to **JUST ASK SOMEBODY!**

Silly women.

Viva la Difference

Periodically, like everyone, Charles and I want to "get away from it all." Wherever that is.

It's of prime importance to me to get *there* rather quickly. I do not blossom during car travel.

Subtle Charles gave me a cartoon once -- it showed a man and woman, dressed in flowing desert attire, riding camels with sand and sky as the backdrop. The man turns and snaps at the woman "Stop asking me if we're almost there. We're nomads, for crying out loud!"

I got the message.

If we owned one, Charles would pack a transport vehicle for these intimate little weekend retreats. Having had a job in college as summer-hire for a moving company, he is THE undisputed resident expert on packing the car. (I'd tell him he was, even if it weren't so. In the big picture, it's not a bad job to allow another to have for the duration of a lifetime.)

For a trip to an adjacent county, items must be wrapped, secured, marked and recorded in an inventory log. As they say, *spontaneous* refers only to combustion where Charles is concerned.

When we travel by car, *I* pack in a hefty trash bag. Always king size and double reinforced. I make every effort to put the heavy objects with sharp edges near the bottom.

Charles, on the other hand, smoothes out even his T-shirts. Heaven forbid a wrinkle in an *under*shirt. He places SMOOTHED jockey shorts in some predetermined, empirically proven *perfect* spot on the T-shirt AND THEN puts athletic socks dead center of the jockeys. This *set* is then rolled up and placed sardine fashion across the bottom of his suitcase. I have actually seen the man RE-roll a set to perfection!

AFTER these items are worn, the process is repeated in reverse for the return trip.

Remember, we've been living together in relative harmony for over thirty years. Amazing.

On occasion I've been known to forget little things on trips like my toothbrush and hormone pills. Charles carries an extra brush and a weeks supply of my pills. He put the pills in a bottle labeled "administer at first sign of insanity."

Pharmacy humor?

Give me that kind of friend instead of a wild fling every time.

Keep On Truckin'

Well, it finally happened.

Charles had been biding his time for ten years. He had been *overtly* pining for my daddy's old truck. For anyone who has lusted for a truck, this will make perfect sense.

Lest you think this just *any* old truck - we're talking 1979, lime green, extra long bed ALL-PURPOSE-TRUCK. 80,000 *actual* miles. A spare tire chained to the cab came with the deal. And if you knew what good care my dad takes of his vehicles, you'd really be impressed.

Unfortunately, the truck was in Texas. WE live in North Carolina.

Delta Airlines let us off real close to the truck. Getting it home was a part of the deal that was in fine print. To Charles, driving the truck home took on all the characteristics of a romantic adventure. The fun of the whole undertaking was lost on me from the beginning.

Remember Charles' moving van days? We played long distance trucker the entire trip back to North Carolina. He'd speed up behind *real* trucks for the sole purpose of flashing his lights - using the trucker code - and tell them goodness knows what. I made sure to never make eye contact as we passed any of the truckers, lest Charles err in his flashing and communicate something regrettable. We even exited once at a closed weighing station. Charles said it was a dry run, just for practice. He was not amused when I suggested we make a temporary sign for the window with our 800 number on it, should anyone have comments regarding his driving.

Day one on the road, we stopped at a truck stop for breakfast. Waiting for our vittles to settle, we browsed through the "store" checking out highly useful staples like bandannas, decorator air freshener for the truck cab and snacks made while the FDA wasn't looking.

We spent the night in a tiny town in Alabama. Swell place. Amenities listed on the rented flashing portable sign boasted hot showers, satellite dish and free parking for semi's. Parking for semi's sealed it as our kind of place.

Charles couldn't get over how lucky we were to be able to combine getting the truck with a romantic vacation. Just the two of us out on the road alone. He mentioned this numerous times (whether I responded or not).

And he still doesn't get it.

Patience

Charles has S E V E N (7) or 𝓗𝓛 | | ... that's VII gray hairs.

Someone remarked that gray hair is simply a sign that one is entering a new phase of maturity, otherwise known as "nattily coming undone." I've been waiting, on occasion patiently, for him to catch up. My hair has been gray for years. The man was still showing his ID at age 35!!

Fortunately, to date, there is no sign of his stockpiling Grecian Formula.

Bifocals, Trifocals ...

Hauling around three pairs of glasses on your person, is a pretty clear indicator that it is high time to invest in serious eyewear. It's irritating and a trifle depressing, I admit.

Singing from a hymnal held by someone two rows up is not always convenient. Glasses take some getting used to. Some of us never do. My current eyeware wardrobe consists of:

Main glasses. Useful for seeing large moving objects like MAC Trucks.

2.5 diopters off-the-rack. Necessary for seeing small immovable objects such as words and numbers.

Sunglasses. Handy for recognizing either MAC Trucks or words/numbers while in the sun. Can be worn *on top* of main glasses or 2.5 diopters for short spells (makes a definite fashion statement.)

Charles refuses to admit that *he* needs glasses. When I get a new pair, he asks that I choose some that are not too feminine. He wears my glasses! We buy the perch-on-the-nose variety five or six at a time. We choose a strength that we both can tolerate. That means one of us can't see quite good enough and the other gets dizzy after peering through them for a while.

The old boy is on his own these days. Last visit to the eye doctor and I pranced out with mono-vision contacts. They fix one eye up with a contact that lets you see MAC Trucks. The other contact lets you see words and numbers! This of course means you see nothing really well ever again. But it is convenient.

Dance Lessons

I love to dance. To me it's as natural as walking. Charles on the other can dance, *but* it's much like they say about a dog walking on his hind legs. He can do it, but ... not very well and certainly not for very long. He approaches a dance floor in much the same fashion he would approach a stand of scrub pines that need to be cleared. He also dances scientifically. Memorizing a formula so to speak. He actually has a file in his computer of a graph sheet with the foot movements mapped out. Once he gets in motion, there's no stopping him, music or no music, partner or no partner.

We recently took a swing dance class. After about 15 minutes I told him to relax. He was crushing my hand.

He said "...look, this is a dance class, it's my feet that we came here to work on. When my feet are taken care of, *then* we'll work on my hands."

He was clearly not caught up in the moment.

I said, "Please smile, Honey, try to *look* like you're having a good time."

He said "We didn't come here to have a good time, we came here so I could learn to dance."

We left early and on the way home decided that I would continue to lead when we go dancing. This would free Charles up to do some of the things he does so well, like cut down trees.

Gaslighting

Charles' tools and miscellaneous stuff in our garage *appear* to be a yard sale waiting to happen. If we wanted to start our own landfill, we'd be off to a great start. He's the proud owner of a 28 year collection of small pieces of non-related pipes, boards and broken furniture. Each item in this vast collection has great potential. This last statement was not original with me.

He switches on an electric tool or two, turns the radio on full blast, harmonizes with Waylon and the boys - he's in 7th heaven. If in his youth he had only had a tree house or a small fort my life would be a lot easier today.

The tool situation was so out of hand that we had to build a shed just to hold the overflow.

In the tool inventory there are currently five retractable tape measurers. Have *you* ever wondered, out of the blue, how wide your window sill is? Have you? Of course not. Yet sometimes without warning or provocation, in the middle of a conversation, Charles will jump up, walk across the room and MEASURE A WINDOW OPENING. Now you tell me what use he could possibly have for that bit of information at that particular moment.

I did see the classic movie "Gaslight." Charles Boyer tried to drive Ingrid Bergman insane by slowly turning down the gaslights and pretending not to notice how dark it was getting. He did this over a long period of time. Come to think of it, this tape measure routine has been going on for several years.

Try Alt-P

I have difficulty getting batteries in a flashlight right end to right end. I have to use a magnifying glass to find the ever important microscopic + and the -.

I've managed only a sliver of competency with my computer. It's alarming to be tottering on the brink of hi-tech. Actually I can *hear* the traffic on the information highway, but have no idea where the access road is.

When I hit the wall with a computer problem, it's not possible for me to verbalize what has happened. There are no words in my brain for these maladies. When the computer fails to proceed, I just pick up the phone and call Charles' voice mail at work and calmly state "computer's possessed." That says it all.

Once, after reaching an impasse with the computer, Charles called and offered to "talk me though" the problem. Offering directions for a molar extraction would not have seemed any more absurd.

He suggested I hit alt P. Alt P? Well, I certainly had no better plan. Darned if the computer didn't start humming again.

"ALT P? Why on EARTH did you suggest that? Instead of shake the monitor, dust the keys or go take a nap?" Alt P?

He said "Oh, it was just a stab in the dark."

In a world where physics, income tax returns and computers exist, it's fortunate we humans have our intelligence in different areas. What a joy to find others to compliment our specific brand of smarts.

Let's hear it for TEAMWORK!

Confirmation

Several years ago Charles and I were confirmed in the Episcopal church. This was a major ecumenical move since Charles had grown up under the tutelage of Jesuits and I had come from one of the original clan of Southern Baptists -- Mississippi Southern Baptists at that. Episcopal seemed a good compromise.

My parents were understandably apprehensive when we invited them to come all the way from Texas for the confirmation service. We assured them that they need not participate in any part of the ceremony with which they felt uncomfortable. At the service, my mother's face was expressionless as the visiting Bishop walked down the aisle towards the altar. He was splendid in his elaborate pointed hat and ceremonial robes. Not your typical Baptist attire. With the Bishop chanting and swinging the incense up and down the aisle, generally fogging up the place -- only my mother's eyes moved. Back and forth, back and forth following the incense. Had a hymnal dropped, she surely would have fled screaming to the nearest exit.

After the ceremony, there was a gathering in the church parlor. My parents still weren't sure what they had just been party to. Most especially my mother.

The bishop, a most pleasant and gregarious man, sensing my mother's discomfort, walked over and introduced himself. "I'm Bishop Frasier."

Without thinking, my mother blurted "I know, I've been watching you. Nobody's ever done anything like this before in our family. I have no idea what I've just been party to. There hasn't been even one hymn I recognize."

Ever the skillful diplomat, Bishop Frasier said "I can understand. I was the first one in my family to do something like this also. I haven't turned out too bad. Your daughter will be just fine."

My parents stayed for a week, and attended church with us the following Sunday. The Bishop obviously had spoken with our parish rector, for ringing through the rafters during the usually solemn choir processional was the unmistakable foot-tapping-congregation-swaying-rattling-the-rafters-hymn "Bringing in the Sheaves."

Our rector gave my mother a quick wink as he passed our pew.

Silence is Golden

After thirty years in a relationship, you *know* there are times to say nothing.

Charles loves electronic gadgets. Big ones, little ones, useful ones, even non-useful gadgets that are a complete waste of time. Matters not. He delights in tinkering with everything from music boxes to garbage compactors. So great is his infatuation with his gadgets that even after they break and then as useless items, start getting in the way, he stores them, "in case some small *part* of them will be useful *some*day."

His office at home looks like the stockroom at Radio Shack. My least favorite of his many electronic toys is a combo alarm clock, radio, barometer, shoe shiner, and wallet holder. It's *his* clock on *his* side of the bed, therefore *his* responsibility to operate it. The high tech feature of *my* clock is that the numbers glow in the dark and it has a non-tipable base.

Once Charles left on a business trip. The clock, with all its cleverness, did not realize he had left. At 6:00 AM just like clockwork (pun intended) the clock, radio, barometer, shoe shiner, sans wallet, started it's routine.

I couldn't shut the *&@%*grrr thing off!

It made me even madder to realize, had there been an elementary school student at hand, my problem would have promptly been resolved. The electronically inept among us steadfastly refuse to believe digitals are here to stay.

Jerking the plug from the wall, of course the emergency power pack kicked in. I hog tied the radio with a pair of pantyhose between two pillows and threw it to the back of Charles' closet.

He returned home, found the clock and to this day has never said a word.

Try It!

I don't know how *many* times you could get away with it but it **did** work.

One night, I broke down and said, "Charles, for over a quarter of a century, I've been giving it my best shot. And today I'm here to tell you, I'm getting sick and tired of planning these meals."

He looked down at his plate and then with total disbelief looked up at me and said:

"You *PLANNED* this!??!"

To say that my meals are not exactly memorable is an understatement. One evening I was deeply engrossed in a *hair-raising who-done-it*. Charles tiptoed in and said "honey, gee ah, I hate to bother you but, ahhh, it's getting late and I was just wondering, mmmmm...did we eat yet?"

Recognizing opportunity I yelled "DID WE EAT YET?!! You don't remember?" He said "Oh yeah -- hey, just kidding, a little joke, catch ya later..."

It worked!

Initial This Banana

I'm not a big eater, but I am interested in having food around in case I do get hungry.

Charles eats a lot. And often. Sometimes even right after he has just eaten. He burns off hundreds of thousands of calories with his projects.

Anyone sharing space with a man knows there's "mine" and "his" and "ours." Food would reasonably fall into the "ours" category ... unless you lived with Charles (which you can't, 'cause I won't let you.) Over the years I've learned it's necessary to write my name on *my share* of fresh fruit, particularly bananas. Before I began this, a bunch of bananas could go from grocery cart to our kitchen counter and disappear in less than 24 hours. The equivalent of a Central American banana plantation's seasonal harvest would pass through our kitchen without my having more than one large bunch. I felt like the go-between for Charles and the banana cartel.

In the pantry I have a dog biscuit box. We haven't had a dog for years. It's for my personal cache of food. Charles asked about the box once and I told him it was for lost dogs that may show up at our door. He bought it ... and fortunately, he has never been *that* hungry.

Kim, now married, has a dog biscuit box too. Paul, her husband, eats a lot and often. And sometimes even right after ...

Cordon Bleu

The old ego hit bottom while driving along listening to a Public Service announcement for the local school lunch menu. Charles turned the radio up and said "doesn't that sound good!"

Being ill-suited to cooking is something I come by quite naturally. I come from a long line of menacing yet well intentioned cooks.

My mother called shortly before we were coming for a visit. She asked "Want any special meals? If so, be sure to bring them with you."

Charles often tells me to stay in bed so he can *get* breakfast.

The key word here is GET. Alas, once again we have differing opinions as to when night ends and morning arrives. As I snuggle back into my pillow, along with the rest of mainstream society, I hear the car racing down the driveway. It's Charles off to GET breakfast.

Apparently morning has arrived for him.

Breakfast in bed means but one thing. Two biscuits, extra strawberry jelly for the little woman and something dark and lukewarm that passes in a pinch for coffee. All this delivered on my very own molded cardboard tray!

Ain't love grand.

A Dollop of Cheese Food

Watch out Julia Child...

I love those gourmet cooking shows.

The cooks seem so *focused.* So confident of what's going to happen. Never do they peer into the fridge mumbling, "Hmmm, wonder what..."

Julia Child is my culinary idol. I could teach Julia a thing or two in the garden, but she's the undisputed queen of kitchendom. I like her style, and her expensive French pots.

A fan once asked her if she ever cooked healthy food. Julia said it wasn't that she actually objected to healthy food. It was just such a bother, when merrily creating a masterpiece, for nutrition to rear it's ugly head.

I've experienced those feelings myself while reading the nutritional info panel on a bag of Cheezie-o's.

Once Julia was preparing a rack of lamb in mint sauce with wild rice and white asparagus. Raptly hanging onto her every word, I was at the same time preparing tuna and noodle casserole topped off with a generous dollop of imitation cheese spread.

I just gotta get some of those expensive French pots...

"Man in the Kitchen"

We have a clear division of labor in our home. Outdated method maybe, but it works for us.

I never tend to a buckling driveway and Charles never sautés. He still refers to our major appliances as the tall-cold-one and the short-hot-one and the loud-wet-one.

Unfortunately, the man has learned the few culinary tricks he knows from me. Early in my career, on an out of town speaking trip, Charles was left in charge of meal preparation.

Upon my return I asked Kim how the meals had been.

"All right I guess" she said.

"Well, what'd you have?" I quizzed.

"Lasagna."

"*WELL*, was it any good?"

"Yeah. OK, I guess, but the beans weren't done."

Aisle 8

Check out your local grocery store. It beats watching planes take off at the airport for low budget entertainment.

Singles go to the grocery store to meet other singles. Hungry people go for food. I occasionally go for a little humor. If you stay alert, trips to the grocery store *can* be worth a nominal admission fee.

With one hand on a grocery cart, people act like they're in a soundproof booth. They will say anything! Figuring, I guess, that the Brussels sprouts will never tell.

In case you are mildly interested, the best action takes place in the produce department. A woman once started an artichoke avalanche. Dutifully, she tried to stop it and got pricked and skewered for her efforts, all the while trying to muffle her embarrassed cries.

Passing the produce weighing scale, an absolutely ancient lady went back, and took a second look at it and then changed her watch!

A cheerful gent sporting brown and green plaid Bermuda Shorts and a Hawaiian print shirt moseyed over to the fresh pineapples. You could just tell this man was law abiding from the word go. To test for ripeness, he started pulling on the leaves of a select batch of pineapples. Unbeknownst to him, the produce man had cut away the tops of some of the fruit, getting them ready to be sliced. The elderly gent picked one of *them* up, pulled at a leaf and the entire top came off. He stood still as a post for about three seconds and then he put the decapitated pineapple into his cart. His expression gave no clue to what was going through his mind.

Charles rarely shops for groceries. If there isn't at least one section of plumbing pipe on his list, he's in the wrong store.

Once I gave him a long shopping list for an upcoming party. He came home from the grocery with bags of bizarre, seemingly randomly chosen non-related items. Even he was perplexed. Thinking there was a mix-up with another shopper's groceries, I loaded everything up and went back to the grocery store. After a little detective work, I concluded Charles had, somewhere along the line, accidentally exchanged his cart for a cart one of the store employees was working out of, restocking shelves.

One of the checkout women said, "You know, we were wondering what that man was up to. But we weren't about to ask. We never have had any one person buy *everything* in the **Reduced For Quick Sale** cart."

True Grit

Charles and I have reached middle-age. OK, I'm excessively optimistic. At any rate, we are sincerely trying to be more health conscious. I am in charge of keeping us on the nutritional straight-and-narrow.

We now buy "roughage" by the pound at the health food store. I don't know exactly what it is, but it's supposed to be good for you. It most resembles the stuff Aunt Reuta Lee used to mix in her chicken feed. (None of her chickens had names.) It looked strikingly like teeny tiny little rocks, and was descriptively called *grit*. Grit is apparently good for what ails you if you're a chicken.

As a child, I thought a diet of *grit* was the reason chickens couldn't fly. Anything would be hard pressed even to move fast, much less gain any altitude to speak of, after eating a full course meal laced with gravel. Come to think of it, it *may* very well be the reason chickens can't fly.

You could switch my all-natural cereal breakfast with Rhode Island Red Breeder Mix and the bowl would be half-way empty before I'd notice something was different. It's easy to understand why chickens are so frantic at mealtime. They want to get that stuff down before their taste buds kick in.

This *may* be good for us, but I'm not yet overwhelmed. Not until the scientific community can create healthy food that routinely tastes like cream puffs will I be impressed with technology.

Filed Under "K"

Kool-Aid organized according to flavor? If that doesn't take the cake.

Charles has tried unsuccessfully to use his influence in determining how the kitchen is organized. He simply refuses to believe there is actually a functioning system *already* in place.

What's your reaction to specific pantry sections:

1. Kool-Aid -
   - a. sweetened
   - b. nonsweetened
2. tomatoes -
   - a. whole
   - b. sauce
   - c. paste
3. popcorn -
   - a. microwave
   - b. stovetop

He suggested those very ideas.

GIVE ME A BREAK!

On top of that, he has hinted that plastic drawer dividers might also be a good idea. They make no sense at all. When one divider fills up, you move on to the next. Can't we assume we have all come to recognize a fork regardless of it's surroundings. Seeing 8 forks stacked in a neat pile does not help me identify a fork one bit easier or faster. So, where's the benefit?

Charles has this thing about lids. Everyone else knows lids are primarily to keep flying "*things*" out of the jar and items from falling in from the shelf above, right? Charles places far, far too much emphasis on the importance of lids. He screws them on like the contents of the jar were headed straight for a time capsule. He actually insists upon using the *very* lid that was on the jar at the store or another one the same size. Picky, picky, picky.

He claims *my* system, unerringly is to place all infrequently used items across the front of the refrigerator shelf and the regularly used, truly indispensable items across the rear wall of the appliance.

So?

Once when I returned from a speaking engagement, Charles surprised me with an *organized* kitchen. This, mind you, was a *favor*.

He even created a computer program for this hi-tech pantry "system." The program also would double as a shopping list. With a single command, my computer screen would display how the peanut butter was holding out.

To date, opening the pantry door and taking a peek has worked fairly well for me. Of course, a computerized kitchen *could* add to excuses for not cooking dinner. "Sorry, we eat out tonight. Electrical storm. Had to unplug the computer...."

Pack Rats

In partial defense of Charles, he IS systematic.

He has in fact, systematically saved AND is in possession of every single item he has ever owned. Well, almost everything.

Once, while in a cleaning and tossing frenzy, I hauled off the entire contents of one closet. It happened on the kind of day when it just wasn't expedient to take inventory of every box. Months after the purge, Charles came running into the kitchen, pale as if he was dangling from a bungie cord.

"It's all gone!"

"What's gone?" I asked.

"I'm not sure, but everything in the upstairs closet is ... gone."

"Yes it is." I responded.

He was FURIOUS even though he couldn't remember anything that *was* in the closet except some 10 year old AAA maps and a petrified golf glove. To this day he's not sure what he lost, but it still makes his blood pressure rise. I suggested that he just pretend we had a small fire and get over it.

I have a good friend, Jeanne Robertson. She has actually added rooms to her home to accommodate her personal, no longer useful, possessions. Her very own child will not be remotely interested in these items upon her demise. In fact, the Goodwill store may not be tempted.

She has shoes that will never again, in anyone's lifetime, come back in style. Jeanne is a veeeerrry tall woman. In her case it makes a little more sense to hang on to things like old shoes. If I wore an 11B shoe, I too might be hesitant to part with foot gear.

She is the most organized person I've ever known. Each useless item is catalogued. I now think long and hard before giving her anything because I know full well that there is a box, file cabinet or dresser drawer already filled with an assortment of like items -- catalogued. After considerable urging, Jeanne decided to clean out a chest of never to be worn again clothing. Hours later, she proudly announced that she had filled up a huge plastic bag with these clothes...and had taken them to the attic.

Unlike most, I have no faded, dried, smashed corsages. No ancient ticket stubs. Even very few old love letters. Maybe I still have those somewhere ... Then again, maybe not.

Helpful?

Charles has made great strides in doing his fair share in the domestic maintenance arena.

Immediately after a meal or a snack, he takes his plate, glasses, and partially depleted serving dishes back to the kitchen.

That's the good part.

Now, try and follow this logic. He *then* places everything on the counter and pushes it waaaay back flush against the counter wall. The container of banana pudding is positioned right there along with the empty glass, used spoon, and milk carton. The refrigerator, pantry and dishwasher never enter his mind as more logical destinations for these items.

He *thinks* he's being helpful.

Surely there is some logic to his exercise. Sometimes I'll return from a short trip and find evidence of more than one meal lined up neatly along the wall. His explanation: "I planned to use most of them for the next meal."

I often wonder, where would this end? What would happened if I were to go out of town for a REALLY extended period. Would he eventually fill up the entire counter? Would his meals be determined by which utensils he had already used and were therefore available on the counter? What would happen if he didn't want to stick with that pattern? Would the neat arrangement inch its way forward to the edge of the counter? ...and then continue onto the floor?

Can you, in your mind, play this routine out over a two week period? I'll have to remember this when scheduling speaking engagements.

Still, to give Charles credit, it is a start...

Mr. Baby Face

Both good news and bad news can be associated with a truth.

Charles looks fully ten years younger than his age. The braces he wore only a few short years ago didn't help one bit either.

That's the truth *and*, some might say, the good news.

The bad news is that I look my age. And that's on a GOOD day, in the RIGHT light.

While enrolling our daughter as a college freshman at Louisiana State University, Charles and I went to the student bookstore for some getting-started-at-college supplies. I asked a student/clerk if he had the adhesive approved for use on the dormitory walls. You know, the kind to stick posters on the wall without doing any damage.

The young man looked at me, looked at Charles, looked back at me and said, "Depends on what dorm he's gonna be in."

At his high school reunion he was voted best preserved. One of his former classmates had the nerve to ask me if I let him date yet.

Agatha Christie handled a similar situation in a most ingenious way. Max, her "later" husband as she referred to him, was both much younger than Agatha and an archaeologist. Agatha said "...smartest thing I have ever done. The older *I* get the more fascinating he finds me!"

Agatha really was into fiction.

Self Improvement

Aunt Reuta Lee didn't *over-do* school. Still, this never has put a damper on her zest for self improvement. An ancient clock resides on the mantel in her living room. There is a drawer in its base and the compartment housing the mechanical workings is gotten to through a door in the back. Whenever she hears a new word that strikes her fancy, she hurriedly runs to get a used Piggly Wiggly cash register receipt and writes down her discovery. This new treasure then gets safely filed inside the drawer in the clock base. Tells time AND stores words. Quite a useful addition to anybody's home.

Think about it. A new word really is a treasure.

Maybe it has been Aunt Reuta Lee who, by her example, has encouraged my commitment to self improvement. Both mental and physical.

Not having errant grasshoppers to chase, I've had to work at getting my exercise. My first encounter with an organized exercise program was with aerobics.

Our instructor was a relatively recent transplant to America. She spoke very little English.

Without a shadow of a doubt, she handily qualified as one of the world's most energetic humans. I needed to take my pulse after she told us what we're going to do in class that day.

It must be strange to learn a new language starting with the major muscles of the body. It would definitely be limiting from a social point of view. *Shouting* this new language would add an even more interesting dimension.

Surely though, it is far more marketable to be able to yell !gluteus maximus! than to whisper in a cavalier fashion "Monsieur, my aunt from Ohio is traveling with a small dog named Felix. What time may we have tea?" Have those phrases from French 101 ever come in handy . . . *for anyone*?

A regular instruction in aerobics class was to "take a deeeeep inhale to the hamstrings - NOW!" It was interesting to observe the variety of interpretations of this command. Some would kick a leg, others would turn around, possibly the wisest in the group would use the time judiciously and just stand still to avoid injury.

My instructor's commands were oft-times hysterical. While doing leg lifts, in a booming voice she would yell:

"SQUEEZE SOME BUTTOCKS!"

Fortunately -- at least every time I'd been in class, everyone made a prudent decision regarding this instruction.

As the World Shrinks

Long before the crumbling of the Berlin Wall, Charles and I were in Budapest, Hungary - *"the Pearl of the East"* - attending an international convention. Not being world travelers, we decided we would take every opportunity this trip offered.

If you've ever seen any Hungarian words, you know that they have some letters we don't have. Quite a few actually. This makes deciphering street signs, and the like, quite interesting.

Day one in the city, with tourist written all over us, we were *detained* for not validating our bus ticket. Supposedly it was clearly stated at the point of ticket purchase:

SOMETHING VERY BAD WILL HAPPEN TO YOU IF YOU DO NOT VALIDATE YOUR TRANSIT TICKETS. RIGHT NOW. RIGHT HERE.

But remember those extra letters that we don't have. For all we knew, the sign said "have a nice day but don't drink the water."

As we bounced along admiring the lovely architecture, a shadow materialized into a man wearing an ominous black leather jacket complete with black beret and black armband. Not even for a moment did we think he was the Hungarian version of the Welcome Wagon Lady. He approached us and started yelling. I asked Charles if we were in trouble.

We were rather roughly led to and then interrogated in a room *under* the subway. Many subways in Budapest were built way underground so they could double for bomb shelters. The location was not mentioned in any of our tourist assistance booklets. I'm pretty sure some spy movies have been filmed in that room. Either that or the events that spy movies depict actually *took place* in the room. There was absolutely nothing in the room except three wooden, straight backed chairs and a hanging naked light bulb.

Interrogated is probably not the best word. Actually they spoke to us using many of those extra letters while we stood scared senseless. And all of this was happening because we didn't validate our bus ticket!

When it finally clicked that **he** was going to continue to speak in **his** native tongue, and **we** weren't getting any closer to understanding Hungarian - **we** gave up. The result was to pay a cash "fine" the equivalent of 1/2 the money we had planned to spend during our week stay. The Hungarian Welcome Wagon Man seemed quite pleased with his meting of justice.

We ate a lot of dumplings and clear broth the rest of the visit. Paprika helped only slightly.

That incident by all rights, should have been adequate for trauma incurred during one holiday. There is more.

Big time world travelers as we were, we bought ONE WAY rail tickets *into* Hungary. The plan was to buy an airline ticket home with local currency once in

Budapest. Such a good idea. We could take a leisurely train ride into the city and then fly to Frankfurt and then home. Once again, naive is too weak a term for this plan. Totally stupid has a more appropriate ring to it.

How easy do YOU think it was in the mid-eighties to leave - at will on a sunny summer's day - from a communist country by air? Air fare for residents of capitalist countries was five times more $$$ than that for residents of a fun-loving socialist country.

Dumb rolled over into scary.

All the English speaking people had obviously left Budapest for the day. We were on our own.

On a map we saw two train stations. Only one station was on tracks that left the country. That station clearly represented freedom. Charles left me at one station to "see what you can find out" while he checked out the other station across the city.

Right.

Alone. No knowledge of the language. The only person for countless hundreds of miles in Nike shoes, L.L. Bean T-shirt and an Atlanta Braves cap. Spanish 101 wasn't going to help one bit.

They say action is better than inaction. At least most of the time. In a variety of situations. Not this time.

I started standing in a line. It seemed to be what most people were doing. Sure were lots of lines to choose from. The woman in front of me had on a babushka, a cloth bag stuffed with bread and the proverbial bottled water and very few visible working teeth.

She stared at me. I gave her my biggest "Hey ya'll" smile. You know how it is to smile at a baby and get no response. She may have been related to the black leather jacketed transit authority we encountered earlier.

The man at the ticket window was an unusually disagreeable shade of gray. This probably developed after numerous years of breathing the breath of so many people yelling into the little hole in the window of his booth. He too may have been related to the woman in line.

It finally was my turn at the head of the line. The agent's unique method of communicating was to repeat his statement just a little bit louder each time all the while moving his lips less and less. This was a technique with which I was unfamiliar. However, not much that had happened thus far was familiar in any way. Finally he pointed to a large map on the wall, indicating that the line I'd been standing in was for tickets to Czechoslovakia.

This would not have been good news for Charles. My parents wouldn't have been too thrilled either.

Six hours later, after a smattering of bribes, numerous tears, and some desperate impromptu mime that would have made Marcel proud, we got our two rail tickets. My ticket was squeezed in a vise-like grip in my sweaty palm. When it came time to surrender it to the conductor, we had to pry my fingers open.

A kindly Hungarian gentleman in our traveling compartment informed us that we would have to give our "left over" or "surplus" Hungarian money to the authorities before arrival in Vienna. Under the circumstances and events of the day, this idea did not appeal to us. With no discussion, we threw our "left over" money out the train window, hoping it would be found by someone walking along the tracks. Someone who couldn't be on the train to freedom.

How Did A Nice Girl . . .

The pearl came off my favorite ring. It was not a gift from Charles.

Having unrolled roofing paper 20 feet off the ground, squeezed caulking around skylights and installed a chimney cap, how hard could it be for me to glue a little pearl back on a post while on level ground? The only difference would be that, with Charles out of town on a business trip, *this* project I'd handle alone.

As with most minor repairs, the first step was a trip to the hardware store. The salesman emphatically recommended a specialty glue so strong, that it allows you to relocate an elephant if there's a helicopter handy. Glue, ring, pearl and I eventually got down to business at the dining room table. To clear a work place, a bunch of clean, unfolded clothes got shoved to one side.

I should have anticipated trouble when the very first step did not go according to plan. Vigorously mashing the tube, nothing came out. Obviously an air pocket. My irritation and aggression grew. Even "encouraging words" yelled at the tube were to no avail.

Then suddenly and unexpectedly, BLAPPPP!!! The *entire* contents of the tube emptied. For a moment I thought the "words of encouragement" had been effective. Then, UH-OH.

Glue droplets were on me, the table and everything on it. I grabbed a cloth from the batch of to-be-folded clothes. Wrong. Now not only were my fingers glued together, they were glued securely to a to-be-folded item.

Now, for quite possibly all eternity, permanently affixed to my person, was a pair of Charles' jockey undershorts.

I tried *everything* to get unglued. Soon, rational thinking resumed and I called the emergency room at our local hospital. As clinically as possible, I explained my situation to the nurse over the phone, only to hear her yell,

"Hey everybody, get a load of this, it might not be such a sloooow night after all."

Regaining professional composure, she suggested I soak my hand in acetone.

We were fresh out of acetone. *Darn. And it was on my list.*

More deliberation and it became clear that I needed to "come on down." Driving through the darkened streets at that ridiculous hour, I tried to get prepared. What would they think?

At the check-in desk the nurse on duty turned around. "Terrific, just terrific." I knew immediately it wasn't the nurse to whom I had explained my situation - as clinically as possible.

Not wanting to waste anyone's time, I plopped my hand and new appendage of underwear on the counter.

She looked at my hand and the underwear for a long time. Then slowly, ever so slowly, one side of her purple raspberry lips curled up as she chortled,

"Awww. He got away didn't he...?"

Lead Usher

Charles and I were on the lead ushers list at church. What this really meant was that we had been ushering so long that we had experienced just about every emergency or quirky situation ushers experience. And of equal if not more importance, we could be counted on to be on time even for the early bird service.

One summer Sunday morning several members of the congregation came up to us, stating that a young man seated on the last row might need a bit of monitoring. Our church is in the center of town and within easy walking distance of the bus station. Word "on the street" is that the Episcopalians make the best *free* coffee in town. This young man was probably just passing through and wanted a break from the bus terminal scene.

By his overall appearance, things had not been going too well. His long hair was in a scraggly pony tail, tied with a piece of string. His clothes had seen many miles since the last tumble in a laundromat. And, while it was a warm morning both inside and out, he had on a jacket. In my imperial position as co-lead usher, I took full responsibility for monitoring this visitor. He didn't make a move that went unobserved. Because of numerous clues, he soon realized "that lady is in charge of *something* at this church."

I could not tell you one thing that went on during the service that day. All my attention was directed at keeping my eye on this "newcomer." It was my self-appointed duty for the mission of the church that Sunday.

Well, the service rolled along in spite of my efforts and soon it was time to take the collection. Temporarily preoccupied while passing the plate, I forgot about my charge. There was a big crowd at church that day and the collection plates were overflowing. As we approached the last few rows, there he was. Still seated right by the open back door. He'd had plenty of time to plot and scheme the entire service so he could grab the money and run out the open door. I could see the headlines now "Dedicated usher struggles with transient while congregation looks on in horror."

What would he do? How would I respond?

One thing was for sure, I couldn't *do* anything until he acted first. Two rows, one row and then the collection plate, all that money and I stood right next to him. No choice but to hand the collection plate to him.

Slowly the stranger reached into his jacket. His hand hesitated just a moment and then he pulled out a worn leather coin purse. With trembling, stained hands, he unzipped the tattered pouch and poured its entire contents -- every bit of 30 cents -- into the plate.

Judge not, lest ye ....

Lizard Tails

Although I don't have enough material on gardening for an entire book I feel this tip to be important.

Proper method for separating and transplanting Bearded Irises: Since the Irises *should* have been planted quite shallowly, they more than likely can be pulled up with a firm tug shortly after a good rain or a liberal soaking. Not to worry if pieces break off. Iris rhizomes, like lizard's tails, will grow back.

Once dry, remove as much dirt as possible. This can best be done holding the plant by the leaves and whacking the rhizome on your thigh. Once thoroughly dry, place rhizomes in a brown bag to which you've added a cup or so of powdered insecticide. Not the weak stuff for fleas, but something with mega-pyrethrums. Put irises in one at a time and shake. A la shake 'n bake. This kills any small varmints and sends a message to those lurking at the new planting site. Rotten slimy parts of the tuber are obviously not good. I do give you *some* credit. Get rid of them in the way most acceptable to you when dealing with rotten slimy parts of anything.

Irises prefer rather poor soil in full scorching sun which may explain why I grow them in abundance. Shallow planting means the soil doesn't have to be broken up very deep. BARELY cover the tuber. I know this will go unheeded. All across America, Irises are miserably over buried. One woman can only do so much.

Water and leave them in peace. No fertilizer for a long time. Even longer than that. Nothing is more grand than a stand of these splendid flowers. Next to peonies, they are the most regal of blossoms. The only pest that seems to bother them is the leaf borer. Prevention of and treatment for the borer will be discussed in a future book.

Possibly.

Lucille

I've had some pretty interesting friends, if I do say so myself. Right up there at the top of the list was an elderly woman named Lucille.

Lucille lived in a big old house on a major thoroughfare in Chapel Hill. We hadn't met but I must have passed her house dozens of times each month for years. Driving past one day, I saw her picking up fallen persimmons. A gnarled persimmon tree stood square in her front yard. The time seemed right to stop by, say howdy, and introduce myself.

I found out she and her persimmon tree had been living there since way back when the highway was a one lane dirt road. Saturday mornings she used to catch a chicken, then go sit on a tree stump with the chicken immobilized in one hand and hatchet in the other. She would patiently wait for the infrequent passer-by. When a car approached, she'd go stand in the middle of the road, chicken in tow, blocking traffic. She would make the person chop off the chicken's head before letting traffic move again. Believe me, SHE could make somebody do this.

Back to the persimmons.

After numerous not too subtle compliments about her fruit tree, Lucille told me to pick a bucket of the delectable fruit. The persimmons were ripe to perfection. "Why, what a good idea!" I exclaimed. Suppressing my smile, I picked as fast as I could while trying to not appear too greedy. Balancing one last fruit carefully atop the others in the bucket, I smugly turned to Lucille to display my bounty. Admiringly she said "Good work. That bucket will be mine. You can pick the next bucket for yourself."

Lucille was smart in a way you don't learn about in school. She knew all about people. She even knew what was going on down at the police station. Her police scanner squawked 24 hours a day. Before walking got difficult for her, she'd go hang out at the station just for a little excitement. When she had to quit driving, I kept her supplied with the Enquirer Tabloid. She liked it, but said it wasn't nearly as interesting as knowing what crimes your very own friends and neighbors were committing.

Being friends with Lucille was educational. For instance, do you carry paper bags and a shovel in your trunk? I didn't either.

She couldn't believe I wondered why. "If somebody wants to give you something how you gonna carry it off without a bag?"

Good point.

"A Shovel?"

"If they want to give you a plant, you gotta dig fast before they change their mind."

Lucille always carried a pocket note pad and a small, chewed up pencil. It was backup for calculator's addition. She said "it only takes 'em messing up one time." Having worked hard all her life, much of it doing "man's work" and growing up poor, she wanted *every* penny accounted for.

In the summer her legs gave out. Then one day they *up and sold* her house. Today a tennis court is where her house used to be. Somebody's jacuzzi foams atop her rotting persimmon roots.

botanica expertivium friendesquii

Louise Smith was a school librarian for many years. She may have even gone to school with Dewey Decimal. To this day, you'd better not ask her if she knows something because, if she doesn't, you can bet she will when she talks with you next. And you'd best use that information too. She can still give tests.

Louise is the only person I've ever known who uses the Latin Botanical names for common flowers like Johnny Jump Ups.

She's a Yankee. The New England variety to be exact. As a lifelong Southerner I can personally vouch for how admirably she adapted to mildew and heat south of the Mason-Dixon. Her roots in New England partially explain her commitment to practicality. A regional motto is "use it up, wear it out, make it do or do without." It's probable she has every button, at least every button not currently on duty, that has crossed her path for the past 40 years.

Never given to dallying, one day Louise decided to move back to the land of thermal underwear, closer to kin. Singlehandedly she packed up and headed north. Far as I can tell, she never looked back. She just does what needs to be done. Watching Louise in action always reminds me of my favorite Kathryn Hepburn story. Supposedly, a passerby saw "Kate" unloading firewood from the trunk of her car. The individual stopped and offered to help. "Kate" gruffly refused, stating that anyone fool enough to drive as far as she did for that small amount of wood, ought to have to unload it all by herself. Louise would agree.

Calling Louise with a gardening problem was like calling the automated computer at the state agricultural extension agents' office. A quick description of a lethargic plant or a suspicious bug would generate a suggested method of action that invariably proved successful. Much of the fun of gardening is gone now that Louise has moved. There's nothing like having a master gardener walk around your garden in early Spring with "ooohs" and "aaahs" over your every effort. Compliments from others are but a good substitute. Although in her absence, I must admit, it's getting easier and easier while walking visitors through my garden, to make casual reference to *viola rafinesquii.

---

* aka Johnny Jump Ups

Pomegranates

People really do eat pomegranates. I'd always guessed they were grown primarily for watercolor painting classes taught at the "Y."

My first opportunity to learn more about this mysterious fruit came while evaluating banana options at my grocery store. Across the isle I noticed an older woman carefully sorting among several pomegranates in a way that suggested she could tell good from bad. Since I'd never seen anyone contemplate this exotic fruit without a paintbrush in hand, I had to ask her "*do you know about pomegranates*?!"

You're probably thinking "There's that shyness coming out again." But it's true. At the grocery and on the speaker's platform are the only two places my shyness is lost. For some reason I most easily meet people in these two places.

Well this picky pomegranate purchaser proceeded to tell me a not too shortened version of her life's experiences with the fruit. And what a life. The most memorable story had something to do with bursting the fruit open in the sleeper compartment on a train, spraying seeds all over the walls and ceiling. I was tickled with the image but I've forgotten how it ended.

Well, Nita Clendeninn and I exchanged telephone numbers, and in a few days she invited me for lunch. Over soup she continued her discourse on the pomegranate and by the sandwich we were well into our new friendship.

If the grocery manager had requested over the public address system: "Shoppers, find another shopper in the store right now, with whom you could most likely become close friends" ... chances are slim Mrs. Clendeninn and I would have chosen each other.

First there was an age difference. Lots'a years. Then there was how, when, and where we grew up. Mrs. C grew up in Harlem during it's golden era. As a child she could step out her front door, look in one direction and see the Polish butcher and the Italian baker, or walk around the block to the famous African American photographer VanDerZee's studio. Her stories tell of streets alive with an exotic variety of sounds, smells, and sights.

Childhood for me in the 50's was in a modest Texas "ranch style" house with a big picture window that looked into a room we never used. The distinguishing feature of my neighborhood was sameness. Everything for miles around was flat and low -- except for fields of huge TV antennas shining in the hot sun like inverted aluminum root systems springing from every house.

On the surface, it appeared Mrs. C and I had nothing in common. But, it didn't take long before we realized we had more in common with one another than we had with many of our other friends. In her youth, Mrs. C squelched her artistic urges, and went to nursing school. I suppressed the desire for a life on the stage, pursuing a liberal arts degree because it was more "versatile." But we both have souls of artists. When Mrs. C was about my age, she took up painting. One of her Mattisse-like paintings hangs above my desk. It's darn good! My own career with a microphone started after the 1st gray hairs. Ms. C's largest file in her home office is a huge box overflowing with pieces of paper. MISCELLANEOUS PAPERWORK is scribbled across the top flap. I too have that filing system. We're bewildered by the very same things.

Who is to say what makes a friend. It can be when we see a bit of ourselves in the other. Or it can be when we see, a bit of what we can never be.

Ideally, it's a bit of both.

Miller

At my last real job, the parking sticker issued for my car authorized a *preferred* space three quarters of a mile from my office. From my office window you looked out onto a concrete alley connecting my concrete building to the adjacent concrete building. Pigeons were fond of my window.

Unquestionably, the most expensive as well as most hi-tech piece of office equipment was an electric pencil sharpener. It broke my first day on the job and my name was misspelled on the door.

Working quasi-subterraneanly was a bit difficult to get used to. However, the pigeons couldn't get in, so I soon adjusted. This job turned out to be one of the best things that ever happened to me. That seems hard for me to believe too.

Shortly after my coming on board, it was announced from on high that I would be teamed up with an older man for the purpose of doing some training programs. Sounded fine with me.

That was before I actually met Miller Harrison. (A little background on this character might be helpful.)

Miller was, *as they say*, resistant ... or more accurately, wholly non-compliant when it came to traditional corporate rules.

Many a time I saw him enthusiastically commit *us* to a clearly defined, time perishable and profoundly important plan of action, only to leave the room and throw the folder with the instructions into the trash can!

It was terrifying to be associated with him. He held my professional future in his hands. And yet, this responsibility didn't seem to concern him. He would say "just pay attention to me and I'll teach you everything you need to know about the world of work." And he did.

Unfortunately, it will not be possible for me to relay many of the lessons. I do want my grandchildren to read this book. I am, however, able to share some of the more important concepts.

#1   Don't automatically assume that just because someone is red in the face and veins are standing out on his/her neck, what he/she is saying is necessarily important.

#2   Refrain from getting into a serious altercation with someone whose ethics fall appreciably short of yours. This rule has been edited considerably for the purpose of the intended "G" rating of the book.

#3   If you can't change your situation, you can always change your attitude towards the situation.

The more I think about it, these are about all the rules one needs to cope adequately with the world of work.

Yes, I learned a lot from Miller. If I'm ever taken to the hospital by a rescue squad, uttering life's lessons in a semi-conscious state, sure hope it will be the *edited* version of what Miller taught me...

Who Were You?

Reunions are traumatic.

Biggest shock of my life was to find out my first heart-throb is a voting member of AARP. The blond curls that in my youth started my heart fluttering at 40 paces have been replaced with plugs of the purchased variety. Sansabelt slacks ride high on the once rippled mid-section of my first passion. Sob.

Somehow growing older never really hits home until you see comrades of your youth *having already done it!*

It's downright unraveling to go to a party and have to wear a picture - PROOF - you are still who you were. AND *still* have people not believe you.

Palm Tree Mentality

When we go on adventurous holidays, faith is our primary planning tool. For a Key West snorkeling trip, we never asked the qualifications of the captain, the sea worthiness of the boat. Heck no. We just wanted to know how much it would cost, would there be cold drinks on board, and what time do we shove off. We started packing our snorkel gear.

The crew of our boat had very little nautical ambiance. I think *none* is what I mean.

The "captain" had a pierced nipple. Further fashion statements were made by numerous symbolic tattoos. I tried not to read them.

He apparently could hear tunes without the aid of a Walkman. To his credit, I must say he seemed in continuously good spirits. When we took a hunk out of the side of the boat upon departure from the dock, he hardly seemed concerned.

We left the harbor and went where "off shore" really means something. It was way out. How do they know just where to stop? Just where the fish hang out waiting for tourists? Beats me.

The whole bunch made me nervous. They didn't act like sailors. Nobody called anybody "Mate." Not once did I hear "Ahoy." And navy blue was nowhere to be seen. They sensed my concern. "Look lady, we do this every day. There's nothin' we don't know about this part of the ocean..."

Well, we had come a long way, paid a lot of money and anticipated the snorkeling a whole lot. It was too late to start thinking sensibly.

By the time we dropped anchor I was ready. Without a moment's thought, I jumped into the inviting blue water.

Greeting me below was a five foot nurse shark. I missed landing on its back by six inches. Remember how **The Roadrunner** used to run off a cliff and then jump right back up in one leap ... With a superhuman leap my flippers were slapping the deck. Casually, I queried our stand in for Jacques Cousteau:

"Should nurse sharks be an issue of concern?"

He said "In my entire career (HE WAS IN HIS 20's!!!) I've never heard of a nurse shark biting a vital part of somebody."

Climbing back down the ladder, I was at a loss to identify a non-vital part of mine.

The next day Charles and I camped on the Dry Tortugas. It's a teeny island about 50 minutes off Key West by sea plane. The entire island is a Civil War fort; that's it, the entire island. The walls of the fort are at the edge of the island. It was clearly a construction job from hell. Dr. Mudd, the physician who set John Wilkes Booth's leg after Lincoln's assasination, was imprisoned there for practicing the Hippocratic oath on a persona non grata.

How romantic. A prison on a remote island in warm blue waters.

Chances are, Mudd didn't have fun there either.

The island has no fresh water, shopping, air conditioning or lounge chairs. Charles decided it would be the perfect place for us to camp overnight.

Camping makes absolutely no sense to me.

Wonder how many times the settlers on the plains reminisced about their sod houses after they moved into a real house. Or, what are the odds that once Mr. and Mrs. Cro-Magnon got their first shipment of PVC plumbing pipe and thermal windows that one of them said "Hey, I've got a keen idea, let's go back to the cave and sleep on the ground for the week-end, just for old times sake!" See?

Charles and I had been talking about renewing our marriage vows. He brought the subject up once on this romantic getaway. You'd think a man who teaches at the college level would be smart enough to have better timing.

Situations and Responses

How clearly I recall the summer I had my first REAL wurst, REAL strudel and REAL beer.

Charles and I spent a month in Germany. Many of the public rest rooms in that beautiful country still have attendants. Being on the move for a month, we saw many public rest rooms. We thought we'd seen it all, until we got to Bavaria.

One southern German community had a public rest room in which a portable radio played a bracing selection of OOOMpapa's. On the lavatories were tiny bottles of freshly cut flowers. Paper towels had been re-folded and carefully positioned on a platter covered by aluminum foil with *every* wrinkle smoothed out. A highly charged lemon fragrance filled the room.

Just as all of this was soaking in, the rosy cheeked, starched aproned attendant in charge came over to greet me; sensible shoes creaking under the weight of their energetic load. She chattered non-stop until I interrupted and apologized for not speaking German.

Smiling she said "Dat's OK. Thank you for coming to see me. Ya'll come back reeel soon, ya." She walked outside with me and waved a grand farewell.

While we cannot always change our situations in life, we can *always* change our response to our situations. (Miller was right.)

Look Again

Look again. Don't be fooled into seeing what we expect to see.

Chapel Hill is a university community with untold miles of winding brick walkways and all those magnificent old trees. It's easy to see why they put a college here.

Walking on the central campus late one afternoon, my reverie was interrupted by - for lack of a better word - *music.*

Turning to locate the source I saw two students closing in on me. Zig zagging all over the sidewalk, veering onto the grass from time to time, sending squirrels scurrying, they appeared a fearless duo. One was pushing the other in a wheelchair. Not wanting to get run down, I gave them a wide berth.

As they approached, I got a better look. The young man in the back "pushing" was laughing and carrying on with a carefree abandon surely he rarely felt. For he was not pushing at all. He was being led. He was blind.

Tightly gripping the wheelchair remote controls, the young man *in* the chair was the driver. As they got even with me this latter-day Mario Andretti looked my way and flashed one of those indomitable smiles reserved for unharnessed youth on the move. No question about it, his expression said, "We are coming through!" They careened around the corner, hauling their portable music with them.

See There!

A particularly unruly little girl was annoying everyone as she ran up and down the grocery aisles grabbing items and darting between customers. Her harried mother had in tow a crying cookie-smeared toddler in the cart. I recently read where grocery shopping with two preschoolers is being considered for an Olympic event. It gets my vote. However, I'm pretty sure I wouldn't stand in line for a ticket to this one.

The little girl was out of control.

A voice came over the intercom saying "Rebecca, please come to the front office immediately."

The child froze in her steps. Her mother calmly said "well, you don't have to go up there this time, but if you continue to act up, they will have no choice but to come get you."

A store employee was named Rebecca too, and a quick thinking young mother with a sly smile and a much more civilized daughter, pushed her cart up the aisle.

No guardian angels for mothers? Don't count on it.

MWF ISO...

For no logical reason, I read the "personals" ads.

Many are actually quite witty. While never tempted to actually *meet* anyone who "advertises" in this particular manner, I would like to offer my encouragement to some of the more innovative of the bunch. Here are my all time favorites.

"...bright, successful lawyer, trim, very boyish 45, much loved by dogs, small children and parents. Seeks smart, slim, attractive, professional woman, w/good sense of humor. Must be willing to lie about how we met."

"...owner sought for a 1950 model male. Good operating condition, no spare tire. Parks in a 6' space. Driven hard but well maintained. Last owner traded down. No liens. Operates smoothly in traffic; uses horn judiciously. Cleans and waxes well for social callings. Uses light alcohol, non-smoking fuel. Garage comes with the deal..."

"...middle-age female smart enough to know long walks on the beach and quiet evenings by the fire don't get the dog washed or the grass cut. IF you're ready for a grown up relationship, we can work out the details..."

"College professor, builds houses in spare time for diversion, avid collector, novice in the kitchen, beginning dancer..."

WAIT JUST A MINUTE!

SMILE!

Some families have straight teeth, some don't.

Our clan is endowed with very nice, large, strong teeth. The lot of them just haven't always been located in the right places.

Naturally Kim got her braces first. All of her Junior High buddies had them. *She* knew what to expect. *She* was no problem. It's almost a rite of passage these days.

THEN Charles got his braces. If you've noticed, not too many post-middle-aged university faculty get braces. Charles was not a good patient. This became clear even to him when he realized he wasn't awarded a lifesize model of his old teeth like all of his junior colleagues in wire. Hearing a grown man whine about head gear and rubber bands popping out of his mouth and how chewing gum sticks to his spacer is rather disconcerting. Each time the bands were tightened, you'd think he was having multiple root canals.

After Kim and Charles graduated from retainers and the dog and cat had their teeth ultra-sound cleaned, it was my turn. But we hadn't anticipated the new roof on our house. Then there was the matter of the fifteen trees that had to be cut down. (Stump removal cost extra.) Next came repairing the drive... In a nutshell, "things" just kept coming up and my teeth remained shall we say, not in the running for an UltraBright ad.

These teeth have been gnawing tootsie rolls with the best of them for a loooooooong time. I was doing quite well without tooth revamping. *So what was the big deal?*

I'll tell you *what was the big deal.* **I always wanted pretty teeth.**

Dr. Clarence Sockwell, DDS par excellence and genius in the world of things located in one's oral cavity, agreed that tooth modification in my case would indeed be a good idea. This is the way they train them in Dental School to say:

"MY LORD, WHAT ON EARTH HAS TAKEN YOU SO LONG TO REALIZE THIS, WOMAN?"

Going to see Dr. Sockwell and his able sidekick, Phyllis, was the highlight of my week for several weeks on end. I would leave his office humming a happy tune through my numb and swollen lips. La de da, la de dum, ta daaaaaaaa I'm getting pretty teeth! Passersby attributed it to the Novocain.

The day the final cap was nailed into place, the last pointy tooth filed into submission, I victoriously left the office. Safe in the privacy of my car, I looked into the rear view mirror and burst out crying. For almost 50 years, every time I've caught a glimpse of my smile in progress, I've mentally rearranged the errant cuspids.

Now the photographers say, "Open your mouth and give me a *big* smile."

And I do.

Room Service

After a dreadful flight delay, a week's supply of fat grams in the form of peanuts in three time zones, I finally arrived at my hotel room. The digital clock urgently proclaimed it was *EE:EE*. It seemed so much later than that. All I wanted was to take a hot shower and go to bed.

No hot water in the bathroom.

Calling the front desk, I testily brought this discovery to the attention of the front desk clerk. A very youthful voice (recent graduate of a customer service seminar no doubt) asked if I'd like for maintenance to come to my room right away.

"Will they be able to do anything about the hot water." I asked.

"Ah, probably not, ma'm." he replied.

"Would the visit be just to pacify me?"

"Hmmmmm, well, yes ma'm."

With growing impatience I said, "I'm not sure that would work. Not tonight."

The young man was obviously being challenged. Then cheerily he said "How about some apple pie a la mode!"

The customer service seminar worked.

You're On Your Own

My first *real* speaking engagement is forever imprinted in my mind. Just like I'd learned the alphabet, I had memorized my talk word for word from "good evening..." to "thank you for having me..."

Ten minutes into my debut presentation - BLANK!

I lost my place. I had no idea where I was, where I'd been and for sure NO idea where I was going. The audience watched me age as I struggled for composure. Thank goodness most audiences are supportive. They *want* the speaker to succeed.

That I was nervous was a given. It was blatantly clear that public speaking was unfamiliar territory for me. I looked imploringly into the sympathetic eyes of a woman seated on the 3rd row. She looked back and silently mouthed -

"...I don't *know*..."

You're Kidding?

It's probably impossible for normal people to understand how those of us who speak for a living can go into unfamiliar communities, immediately be a part of some never before attended gathering *of total strangers*, yet predictably adjust to whatever unexpected event we encounter. All while guaranteeing to entertain, educate or inform.

Speakers routinely compare notes regarding horror stories that have occurred while on speaking engagements. Here's one.

Rocky Mount, North Carolina is not quite two hours from home. With good roads all the way and no traffic, I arrived for a speaking engagement with a good bit of time to spare before the group was to gather for the reception. As always, a quick check of the room and sound system was a first priority. Walking into a large meeting area, I took a quick look around and announced in a booming voice "*THIS* will *never* do."

The set-up was dreadful. A standing lectern was positioned under one weak ceiling light, barely illuminating the spot where the speaker was to stand. Tables were spread all over the room. There was a movie screen that was the apparent focal point. In a nutshell, it was *not* a setting conducive to good audience interaction with the entertaining guest speaker. Namely me.

Fortunately, there was time to make adjustments before everyone arrived. Rounding up all the hotel staff within earshot, I started shouting orders like a drill sergeant. After much hustling, the tables were rearranged, lectern removed, movie screen carted off and house lights up. The room looked more like what I wanted.

A crowd had quietly gathered at the back of the room. Nobody said anything throughout my hasty set change. As I stood admiring my handiwork, a woman from the crowd calmly walked up to the front of the room and unfurled a large banner. With the assistance of another woman, they taped it to the wall. It read BIRDWELL FAMILY REUNION.

"What? Birdwell? Family reunion?" I choked. "This isn't the Nutrena Sales' annual banquet?"

An African-American woman who was barely able to contain her laughter said "We were sure wondering what branch of the family *you* came from."

Milestones

Milestones are a part of life.

The day I booked a speaking engagement in Fargo, North Dakota was **A Milestone**.

I was psyched. Most of my speaking had up to that point been limited to our southern sisters bordering North Carolina. Cities with familiar names like Cheraw, Alpharetta, and Opelika. Fargo is *practically* out of the country.

My client in Fargo had never had a speaker from as far away as North Carolina. It was a big deal for them too! There was bound to be a swarm of photographers from the media waiting on the ground in Fargo. I kept trying to remember which side is my "best" side and practicing smiling and talking at the same time. It was a long, tiring flight into Fargo. One doesn't just swing by Fargo. I'm pretty sure it's not on the way to anywhere. As the plane was making its final descent, I started imagining the crowd gathering on the ground, shoving for a better vantage point, possibly even placing small children on Dad's shoulders. Boy, this being a mini-celebrity is something I would have nooooo trouble getting used to.

We deplane. The terminal was quite full.

No banner heralding

"WELCOME Linda Pulliam"

No roses.

No swarming photographers. My "best" side wasn't coming in handy. In fact, there was not just a whole lot of interest in me *or* concern about what I was doing in Fargo.

The crowd herded past baggage claim and funneled out to curb side pick up. Just me left. Thirty minutes later, it was clear the Fargo scene was *not* panning out as scripted. I no longer had a best side.

No plan "B" for Fargo.

Moments before calling Charles in North Carolina and asking him to come get me, a tiny speck appeared on the horizon. (You *can* see tiny specks on the horizon in Fargo.) It grew and grew into a HUGE truck.

HUGE truck as in **really HUGE**. This breed of truck jumps competitively over other vehicles in states like Georgia. You can see reruns of world class events starring these huge trucks on cable Saturday mornings. Just ONE tire on these trucks has more rubber than the whole fleet of Chapel Hill taxis. Maybe even with spares included.

The truck looked like a hippopotamus looks when it has been wallowing in the mud. Even the windows were laminated by a veneer of dirt. Windshield wiper tracks were the only sign it was inhabited. Horns formerly belonging to something of a bovine ilk rode prominently on the hood.

Rolling to a stop right in front of me, the cab door opened and a cowboy whose circumference matched his tires got out. To coin an unknown wordsmith, "He was one hood ornament shy of legally requiring mud flaps and backup lights..."

Molded to his head was a cowboy hat. His feet sported boots made from a non-endangered species. His hand tooled belt sported a silver belt buckle that hadn't seen the horizon for a long time. He started towards me.

Shifting his snack from one cheek to the other he mumbled one word: "Speaker?"

Speechless, I responded with rapid head nodding.

Without further cordiality he turned, got back into the truck and started the engine! Kissinger's words rang in my ears simultaneously with the roar of the truck *"The absence of alternatives clears the mind marvelously..."*

Throwing my bags into the truck bed I *crawled up* into the cab. Livestock feed covered the floorboard. An odor quite possibly connected to the horned creature on the hood filled the air.

You don't need a Ph.D. in psychology to read some people. For the next one and one half hours we drove in complete silence. The man was not a talker.

We finally arrived at the location where I was to speak.

My "stage" was the back of a flatbed truck. The special sound equipment shipped in *just* for the occasion was a pair of speakers the size of washing machines. They were propped up on pallets on either side of the truck.

Since it was a farm equipment show, appropriate attire was required. Bandanna handkerchiefs, overalls, tractor caps...

I spoke in the afternoon. Early the next morning we retraced our steps. Same guy; same truck. This time, I had the routine down pat. One and a half hours later, in total silence, we pulled up at the airport. Thanking my driver, I reached for the door.

Without even looking my way he asked

"Hey, does your husband know what you do?"

Rare Indeed

It's true, after people have been married for a certain length of time they DO start to look like each other. An "expert" on television said it was because they mimic each other's expressions and eventually the facial muscles change to accommodate these expressions. Sounds plausible.

At any rate, we do get pretty familiar with our significant others. Once at a banquet, where I was to speak, my seat at the head table was next to the company's CEO and his wife. We were all eating quite uneventfully when the husband (aka THE boss) reached over to his wife's plate and nabbed her roast beef!

With not even the slightest hint of remorse, he proceeded to carve away as if it had always been his. With similar calm reserve, his wife reached over and rescued her slab of meat. On his second attempt to plunder said entree', his wife pointed her fork at him forebodingly, in a decidedly defensive posture.

ALL THIS WAS TAKING PLACE BEFORE 500 PEOPLE!

How embarrassing. To all of *us*, that is. The CEO and his wife never realized what had just taken place. You can be sure nobody ever said anything about what we had just witnessed.

We continued carving away quietly. But I did move my plate a little to my right....

California

After being in attendance for two California earthquakes early in my speaking career, I was booked to return to the State. The way I saw it, two earthquakes is a-plenty for anybody not a bona fide resident of "the Golden State." I've always lived in the land of very still red clay. Let me tell you, shaking earth is scary beyond belief. I'd had my quota.

After arriving in Long Beach and settling into room 1044, I had only fleeting thoughts of my two earlier visits and tucked in for a good night's sleep. Not to be. Before dawn the bed began to rock and closet hangers began to clank.

"Ohhhh nooooo, nooooot agaaaaain."

I had made it just in time for what is now recorded as the most powerful earthquake in 40 years.

In less time than it takes to tell you about it, I was down 10 flights of stairs, touching only about 10 steps, without missing a lick. Pink foam curlers not fast enough to keep up, were left in my wake.

Other scared foreigners assembled outside in the parking lot. There was an older couple from South Carolina, young honeymooners from Tennessee, a wild eyed woman from Alabama and Chicken Little herself representing the great state of North Carolina. To put our terror in perspective, we were *all* used to seeing natural disasters coming on CNN ... with the exceptions of mildew and kudzu.

We later found out the worst thing to do in an earthquake is to go outside. To run like crazy seemed like a good idea at the time.

Later that morning I was seated at the head table commandeering my nerve, preparing to speak to less than half the original number of registrants at a convention. Cowards left.

Almost imperceptibly at first, then - "Yes sirrrreeeee, the water in that pitcher is most definitely moving.

You know how dogs look away from something and pretend they didn't see what they just saw? I tried it. Didn't work.

Soon water was sloshing onto the table and the chandeliers were shaking, making so much noise we had to yell to be heard. The meeting planner said "relax, we've got the strictest earthquake building codes in the country..." Who else needs them!!! He apparently thought that would be a comforting bit of information. It only made me want to be in one of those lax states even more ... like North Carolina, for example. I couldn't wait to hear his idea on how we were to get 400 people under the 4 door openings. Though it didn't help much, the aftershocks didn't last long.

Immediately after the opening session, I dashed to a phone to try and change my airline ticket for an earlier flight. Not an altogether original notion. In fact, the airline agent laughed. Seems the majority of the travelers to Orange county had the same thought, only much earlier.

There was nothing to do except go back to my room and wait for my scheduled flight. My nerves were frayed. Next to the bank of elevators in the lobby, a man from housekeeping had his back to me polishing a brass wall. I pushed the up button then breathed a sigh of relief.

About that time his beeper went off.

I SCREAMED at the top of my lungs. This triggered a similar response in him. He screamed.

I screamed a second time.

The elevator door opened, I quietly got on and never said a word to the poor fellow.

Once in my room, I called Charles. Our son-in-law was spending the weekend with him and answered the phone. I gasped "Paul, I've just been in an earthquake. Is Charles there?"

I heard Paul yelling "Charles, it's Linda. She's been in an earthquake. Can you come to the phone?"

Long silence.

"He's on the roof. Is there a number where he can call you back? He's almost got the gutter fixed."

Well in retrospect, it WAS just an earthquake. That gutter has needing fixing for over a year...

AGHHHHHHHHHHH!!!

Mind Reading

Scene: conference room somewhere in
              corporate America...
Time: early in my speaking career...

In my (required costume of the day) non-threatening gray suit, I nervously await the arrival of the seminar participants. Lacking enthusiasm, they file in, sit down, cross their arms and look at me as if to say, "I'm here. I'm staying 'til you're through. But don't expect a whole lot from me."

This I did not take seriously, for I have had a teenager.

These individuals had not come voluntarily. The session was an upper management sanctioned, mandatory event. Remember how school children respond to having to stay inside for recess as punishment for some minor infringement. Same atmosphere.

After interminable minutes of a one woman monologue, I put my notes down, look at the group and say, "I can do a lot of things, but I cannot read your minds!" To which one man seated in the back of the room replied, "You have got THAT to be *mighty* grateful for."

Who, Me?

At a convention banquet where I was to later speak, it was my pleasure to be seated next to the mother of my client, who was an exceptionally spry *80 something*. While very respectful of her age, I really didn't give her due credit. She was as sharp as tacks.

During the first course, my bread dive bombed into my soup. French Onion soup droplets splattered from collar to cuff. Ever the sophisticate, I yelped and started frantically grabbing napkins from around the table and dunking them into water glasses. This was a brand new silk jacket. The bill had not even arrived yet! After drenching, blotting and dabbing away for a few minutes, I stretched the jacket tautly over my soaked bosom to survey the damage.

My geriatric dinner companion had remained silent. At the end of my ranting, she casually asked "Get it all off?" Rolling my eyes out and downward as far as was physically possible, I replied, "Gee, who knows, I can't see too well."

She continued eating. Clearing the runway for her dessert, she asked "Have you had implants?"

"IMPLANTS??? You mean, to enhance my, er, ah, no Ma'am. Hey, gee, if I'd spent THAT kind of money for some ah, er, well, you know, I'd sure gotten my money's worth, not these ..."

She piped up, "Well I did. Got em both done. Smartest thing I've ever done. Added years to my life."

I was speechless. She was even more "with it" that I'd imagined!!!

Licking her spoon she said "Yep, young as you are, you ought to look into 'em. Get a lot of mileage at your age. Why, now I see even better today that I did twenty years ago."

Out of Body Experience

Everyone has embarrassing moments. We all know that.

When these moments occur when one is standing in front of 650 people, it far transcends embarrassing.

THE worst experience to this point in my life was when I was speaking at an awards banquet for a company that will remain named MUD. One D.

Go back with me...

People were sardined into a huge old dance hall. It seemed especially crowded due to the fact that most of the men were wearing caps and most of the women were wearing fingernails.

My first inkling of pending doom came when the CEO announced "*the woman speaker is 'bout ready to start talkin' so you better make 'nother run to the bar.*" They had been making a "run to the bar" for the past two hours! In fact, it had evolved into more of a weaving shuffle to the bar.

Oh well," I thought, "Maybe the sober ones will sit close to the front."

Wrong.

The man who introduced me asked us to bow our heads for moment of silence for dear old John. Some stayed bowed for the balance of the evening. He assured the highly aromatic group that *"we'll shut this down early so those of you who hadn't yet, can run on by the funeral home."*

The MIC was on a short cord approximately 25 feet from the first row of tables. The overhead light where I had to stand was out. You realize this meant near darkness. Total darkness would have been an improvement.

Before I got 10 words out of my mouth, an older man seated at one of the front tables took out his hearing aid, placed it on the table and promptly started snoring. Another chap, clearly also needing a nap, was carried out over the shoulder of a co-worker. It dawned on me - "Hey, I'm the only thing standing between this group and a really swell time!"

I found out, *trying out a speaker* was a cost cutting measure. Always before they'd had a band and drawing for items such as a big screen television, riding lawnmower, and genuine diamond ring. It's highly likely a few of them were a might disappointed at having a middle-aged woman tell funny stories.

Charles came with me so he could video my speech. I was sure I had sized the situation up accurately when about half way through the speech Charles started packing up the camera.

With much on the spot editing, I finished my presentation in record time. A vestige of my former self collapsed into my chair. Charles leaned over and whispered "I'll go get the car and meet you at the side door." Great idea, however we knew we must stay until the bitter end.

Finally, **Hallucinating Harry the DJ** started spinning tunes. Harry's choice of an opening tune revived a couple seated at our table. Amazingly, they managed not only to stand but to move in a manner implying nominal control. After one particularly energetic twirl, the woman's strapless dress strayed about 10 degrees off orbit. Her bosoms remained at their original location. Blissfully unaware of her exposure, the couple continued to pulsate to the music. Unfortunately, Charles had already put away the camera.

I Hate To Tell You

I am not photogenic. This is not news. Still, it's amazing how compelled people are to share this observation with me.

In preparing new promotional materials, literally hundreds of photos must be taken. Positively grueling. We were on the verge of taking a nose from one shot, eyes from another, creating a composite. FINALLY got one we liked, a little.

We mocked up a rough brochure and I went to a trusted colleague for an honest opinion.

"Well, what do you think?" I asked.

"Linda, I don't know how to tell you this. Sure would hate to see you put any money into anything you'd regret. You know those paraffin Dracula teeth you stick on your own teeth at Halloween? You didn't by any chance have any of those on did you?"

After evaluating the value of our friendship and deciding it was worth salvaging, I explained how hard it is to get a good photo of me. For evidence, I even presented a stack of reject photos.

In an admirable but unsuccessful attempt to recover she said "You know the teeth aren't really that bad, and they *do* keep you from noticing your hair..."

Give 'em the slip

I have heard many women swear and declare this happened to them. I am here to tell you:

I SWEAR AND DECLARE THIS HAPPENED TO ME.

So there.

You choose whom you want to believe. If you hear someone claim this event, check out her waist:hip ratio. Remember the law of gravity. If this person needed to be standing on her head for her slip to FALL down, question her story.

After many years working with institutionalized populations, I made the small jump to corporate America. It took a while to understand the unique behavior patterns of this new group. But after a while, the corporate crew became rather predictable.

At a fortune 500 company, I was conducting a seminar for a group of stuffy managers. In they filed, upwardly mobile suits, leather lunch boxes and Italian loafers - to the foot. In keeping with the mood and tempo that had been established long before I arrived on the scene, I slid into my most "formal" behavior.

Writing on the board, my back was to the group. The safety pin holding together the elastic in my half slip opened, allowing my slip to fall into shackles around my ankles. Panic. What to do? I tried to die. You know you can't die just like (fingersnap) that.

Slowly turning and in a tone of voice reserved for such occasions, I asked "Do I have your attention?"

Granted, it wasn't one of my greater flashes of genius. But it worked.

From that moment on, the group miraculously turned into delightful human beings. In fact, the experience worked so well, I've often wondered how I could rig a trick slip and have it ready for those tough audiences just in case...

In Closing . . .

In committing these memories to paper, one thing is now quite clear. In the half century span of my lifetime, it's the seemingly ordinary events that stand out. Sure, getting up for a paper route at 3:30 in the morning with a baby in diapers was at the time a hassle of major proportions. (THAT comes as no surprise to anybody!) Still, the memory of those struggles are so sweet today. I wouldn't change one thing about my life thus far. For every "inconvenience" there has been an accompanying laugh. For every dilemma, a corresponding rejoicing with the resolution.

Put your own recollections to paper. You may discover that your life and all it's ups and downs have been far more joy-filled than even you thought. I can promise you that your friends and family will be delighted with your efforts.

Most of them anyway...

*That's
Charles*

Order Form

(please print)

Ship to:

NAME: _____

ADDRESS: _____

CITY: _____ STATE: _____ ZIP: _____

☐ GIFT   MESSAGE: _____

_____copies of *A Chicken Named Ruth* @ $12.95 each $_____
Postage and handling:
$3.00 first book; $0.50 each additi~~onal~~
North C~~aro~~li~~na~~

"A CHICKEN NAMED RUTH"
only $12.00 (S+H included!)
Just drop a check in the mail to
Linda Pulliam
863 Weaver Dairy Road
Chapel Hill, NC 27514

.... .o. AHH CAPPELLA PRESS
P.O. Box 16575
Chapel Hill, NC 27514

Ask about bulk rates.   Allow three weeks for delivery

 Call **919 • 942•7348** to inquire about Linda's
availability for speaking engagements.